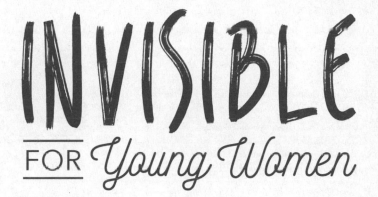

INVISIBLE

FOR *Young Women*

JENNIFER ROTHSCHILD

HARVEST HOUSE PUBLISHERS
EUGENE, OREGON

Cover by Harvest House Publishers Inc., Eugene, Oregon

Cover photos © Darrin Henry, Jo Ann Snover / Shutterstock; DonNichols / iStock

INVISIBLE FOR YOUNG WOMEN
Copyright © 2016 by Jennifer Rothschild
Published by Harvest House Publishers
Eugene, Oregon 97402
www.harvesthousepublishers.com

Library of Congress Cataloging-in-Publication Data
Rothschild, Jennifer
Invisible for young women / Jennifer Rothschild.
   pages cm
ISBN 978-0-7369-6575-0 (pbk.)
ISBN 978-0-7369-6576-7 (eBook)
1. Bible. Hosea—Criticism, interpretation, etc. 2. God (Christianity)—Love—Biblical teaching.
3. Young women—Religious life. I. Title.
BS1565.52.R68 2016
224'.606—dc23

                                                              2015023106

Printed in the United States of America

          15 16 17 18 19 20 21 22 23 24 / VP-JH / 10 9 8 7 6 5 4 3 2 1

Contents

To my nieces
Justine and Juliet Jolly

#worthit

Sarah smiled at herself in the mirror and wondered, *What in the world is going on?* Her day had started off on a pretty terrific note. She'd popped out of bed the first time her alarm went off. She had even laid out her clothes *and* packed her backpack the night before. She—wait for it—ate breakfast, and not just any breakfast! She had oatmeal and some OJ instead of the usual granola bar and bottle of water her mom handed her as she flew out the door. It was going to be a good day. Sure, it would be a busy day—Spanish test, play rehearsal, and Bible study—but she liked being busy. It was who she was. Sarah was a good Christian, a good friend, and a good girl who got good grades!

When she got to school and saw her BFF, Makayla, she noticed how cute her friend looked...again. Makayla always wore the latest styles and had her braces for only a few months before they'd been removed to show off a sparkling white smile. Sarah, on the other hand, was heading into her fifth year of braces with no end in sight. *And why does Makayla have to have such perfect skin too?* Sarah suddenly became completely self-conscious. *I wonder if anyone can see this dumb pimple on my chin*, she worried.

When Señora Sanchez handed out the Spanish tests, Sarah's early morning confidence took a dive. *Unit six vocabulary test?* Sarah panicked. *I thought we were supposed to study unit five vocab!* Glancing around, Sarah saw the rest of her classmates effortlessly filling in all the blanks on their tests. *There goes my A*, she thought. #epicfail *At least I have the play to look forward to.* The drama club had recently held spring play auditions, and all Sarah's friends assured her she was a shoo-in for the main role. Sarah was a good actress—everybody said so. She felt that her voice lessons had been a big help in auditioning for the starring role since the play was a musical.

But when she walked into the theater after school and saw the crowd around the newly posted cast list, Sarah's heart sank. Everyone was saying "way to go" and "congratulations" and "you deserved it" to her main competition, Chloe, who also had perfect skin and no braces. #epicfake

When Sarah finally made her way to the cast list, sure enough, Chloe's name was right next to the starring role—the role Sarah wanted. Sarah's role? Villager. *It's perfect for a good girl with not-so-good grades, braces, and a giant zit on her chin!* she thought to herself. *This is going to be just another face-in-the-crowd role. I might as well be invisible.*

At that point, it was a good day gone bad. Sarah knew she should go to Bible study. She could tell her friends all about her rotten day, and it would feel so good to vent. But as she played the scene in her mind, she realized how stupid it would sound: *I'm jealous of my friend because she doesn't have braces anymore. I was the only idiot who studied the wrong Spanish vocabulary words. I felt so awkward looking at the cast list when everyone else was congratulating Chloe.*

So instead of going to Bible study, Sarah stayed home. She told her mom she had to catch up on her Spanish (which was true!), but in reality she was just done with not measuring up to her friends and classmates. She considered reading her Bible, decorating those picture frames she'd bought at the craft store with washi tape, and beginning that devotional she'd gotten for Christmas.

But after she ate dinner, showered, and studied for a little bit, Sarah found herself reaching for her phone. *Just a little social media before I start on that new devotional,* she told herself. *I'll just see what's on Instagram for five minutes before I study my Spanish.*

Five minutes turned into ten minutes and then an hour as Sarah scrolled through her Instagram feed, scrutinizing the photos of her friends. *Of course there's Chloe striking a pose next to the cast list! Man, just look at all the comments. Everyone loves her! No wonder I didn't get the role. Makayla's smile always looks so perfect. I wish I was as pretty as she is. Everyone's always saying how gorgeous she looks. Wait! Makayla and Caitlyn went out for ice cream together? I wonder why they didn't invite me?*

Sarah's devotional sat unopened on her nightstand as she continued to search through the photos and comments. Noticing that her battery was about to die, she plugged her phone in and headed to the bathroom to brush her teeth—such a chore with braces!—wash her face, and put on Clearasil (which probably nobody else had to use!). And that's when she looked in the mirror and asked herself again, *What in the world is going on? I'm usually pretty upbeat about stuff. I know I'm not perfect, but why am I feeling like such a nobody all of a sudden? Everyone else is so smart and beautiful and talented— and then there's me, Sarah the invisible!*

Have you ever felt like Sarah? Girl, I know I have! I'm a grown-up woman, but even to this day, I have those moments when I'm uncomfortable with everything about myself. I'm even prone to social media anxiety—and I'm supposedly a well-known author! In fact, I remember a miserable road trip to a gorgeous lake, which was actually one of my favorite places (I know, it should have been an amazing road trip!). On that trip, I was bombarded by radio ads and talk shows that reminded me how much more attractive and successful I could be if I bought this cosmetic or tried that workout. Totally focused on me, myself, and I, I did the worst thing ever when I got to the lake. I hopped on Twitter and Facebook and started comparing my posts with the posts of my friends—especially other authors and speakers like myself. Talk about feeling like a failure!

If you're looking for it—if you're 100 percent focused on your own shortcomings—it's easy to find someone else who seems so much better than you are. And sure enough, that's what I discovered. These friends of mine had *way* more followers than I did. While I can only manage to tweet once or twice every two days, these women seemed to tweet up to 12 times a day. I know this because I counted. You've done the same thing, right? (Remember, we're being honest here!) My friends are perfect! They have a presence on Pinterest. You can find them illuminating Instagram. They're brilliant and busy, put together and perfect. How perfect? Many of the friends I was comparing myself to blog every day. E-V-E-R-Y-D-A-Y! Seriously, sometimes I don't even shower every day. (That's not something I would tweet. #gross)

Now, here's something you need to understand. Because I am blind, navigating social media is just plain hard for me. Even though my iPhone talks to me, social media apps, like Facebook, aren't always easy for someone who can't see. For me to spend my time clicking and tapping until my knuckles were swollen and my fingertips were raw just shows how obsessed I was with myself. Of course, I'm not always like this, and I know you aren't either. But we all have those moments when we're desperately trying to discover who we are and how we fit in with everyone around us. And when we fall into the trap of comparing ourselves to others—especially other females—it's easy to find ourselves falling short in just about every category.

No matter how popular you are, someone else will always seem more popular. No matter how good your grades are, someone else will always score higher on an exam. No matter how talented you are, someone else will always seem to outshine you. Measuring your success by comparing yourself to others does nothing more than make you feel like a nobody!

Now, I know you don't want to feel like a nobody. None of us do! But sometimes you just can't help it. The more you think about yourself, the worse you feel about yourself.

When you compare yourself to everyone else, you're going to end up feeling invisible.

Girl, that's what this book is all about—getting yourself out of the "me versus her" mindset and getting into the "God and me" mentality. After all, there's really only one "like" that matters—the "like" you get every second of every hour of every day from God.

It's Not Your Fault!

It's tempting to look for a quick fix for the invisibility problem. I could tell you to stay off social media. I could encourage you to unplug your television and turn off your computer. I could even warn you not to go to the mall or the movies. But we both know that avoiding all forms of media is hardly realistic.

And while it's tempting to rant and rave that Facebook and Twitter will do nothing but shred your self-esteem, which, by the way, they will if you let them, that's another unreal expectation. Besides, media—social and all forms otherwise—isn't the problem. Media simply *reveals* the problem.

> Media isn't the problem—
> it reveals the problem.
> Who I am is based on who He is.

Let's go back to my own Facebook freak-out. Seriously now, how did I ever let myself go there? I was a Christian, for heaven's sake! I knew—really *knew*—that God loved me. I completely understood that I was valuable to Him, no matter how many Facebook friends I had. There was no doubt that my identity was in Christ. So how could an identity crisis hit me—and hit me so hard?

It's true that my identity was—and always is—in Christ. But at that moment, it felt like my identity was defined by an image on a screen and a silly set of numbers—how many followers I had, how many "likes" I'd received, and how many people had retweeted me.

But wait! Isn't who I am based on who He is? And if it is, then why was I even trying to find myself in the first place? If I find Him, I find myself. If I really believe that God sees me, I'm never invisible.

So why even let myself go there—to that place where I'm wrapped in insecurity and invisibility? Here's why: It's because I am *prone to wander*.

As humans we're all prone to wander. We're just one negative thought or comment away from rejecting the truth that God accepts us for who we are and believing the lie that He accepts everyone *except* us. We believe this lie when we put down our devotional, stop seeking God, and get sucked into social media, where we search for other people and see how we compare to them. And then we begin to base who we are on how we feel about ourselves instead of on how God feels about us.

Every girl on this earth has those moments when she finds herself wondering why she doesn't measure up to her own—or someone else's—idea of who she should be.

Now, I want to get something straight. It's not your fault that you're prone to wander. Let me repeat that. *It's not your fault!* It's your human nature. *All* of us have that nature. Every person on this earth is prone to obsess about me, myself, and I. Every person on this earth is prone to wander away from God. Every person on this earth has moments when they find themselves wondering why they don't measure up to their own—or someone else's—ideals.

How many times have you wasted time comparing yourself to others? How many times have you looked in the mirror and thought, *I'll never be good enough*? How many times have you wondered, *Why do others seem to have it so much better than I do?*

Take a little bit of time to think about your answers. You can even write them down in a journal or talk to a friend, parent, or youth leader about them. As you do this, I'm going to introduce you to a young woman who had an identity crisis of biblical proportions. Talk about being clueless about her worth! She was loved beyond belief—loved with the kind of love that only seems to show up in fairy tales—but that wasn't enough for her. She rejected her God-given identity and went with what the world had to offer. And the result wasn't pretty!

"Hosear" and "Goma"

Ever heard of them? I first heard about this couple from my dad, who was the best storyteller ever! Growing up, I loved the way Dad wove together tales that blended a lot of God's truth, a little bit of imagination, and a whole lot of Southern drawl. In fact sometimes I had no idea who he was talking about because their names were lost in Dad's slow, sweet Southern twang.

When my dad told me the story I'm about to tell you—a love story about a totally unlikely couple—I thought the characters were named "Hosear" and "Goma." For real! (Years later, I realized that their actual names were *Hosea* and *Gomer* and that not all storytellers had a Southern twang!)

Hosea (not Hosear) was a young preacher, a prophet actually, who lived in Israel at a time when people weren't interested in hearing his message. Just imagine hearing from God day after day and being given the huge responsibility to tell everyone around you what He is saying. And then imagine nobody listening to you! Instead of listening to Hosea (which they should have done!), the Israelites were walking around with their headphones on, staring at their smartphones, totally tuning out God's messenger. (Not quite, but you get the picture.)

One day God surprised Hosea with a radical message: Hosea's bachelor days were up! It was time for him to get married. And the woman God had picked out for him was simply stunning. Good news, right? Well, maybe.

The good news of Hosea's wedding came with some bad news. His new wife was going to break his heart. She was going to leave him.

Yikes! At this point Hosea might have wanted to tell God, "Thanks, but no thanks. I'm going to find someone else who isn't going to end up hurting me." But Hosea trusted God. And so after his wife broke his heart, Hosea picked himself up, dusted himself off, and did the unthinkable—he forgave his wife and brought her back home because in the end he truly did love her.

Love can overcome anything, even that which seems lost forever. (See, I told you this story was like a fairy tale!)

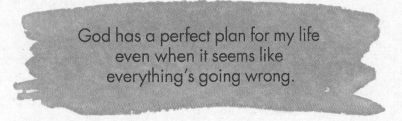

God has a perfect plan for my life even when it seems like everything's going wrong.

The story of Hosea and Gomer is a love story from long ago. When we read it, we see the perfect plan God has for our lives—even when it seems like everything's going wrong.

Did you know that the story of Hosea and Gomer is also your story and my story? It's a story about finding your identity in the perfect love of God and about discovering the *real* you and finding out that you are never invisible. You do matter. You matter so very much!

The girl in the story, Gomer, didn't want anything to do with her husband's love. She wanted something more...something more exciting, something more daring, something that made her feel more like she was *somebody*. Hosea's love should have made her happy, but Gomer was only considering herself.

Now, Gomer had a pretty rough background. As you'll find out, her family situation wasn't good. And the culture of the time didn't help things. Chances are you're probably thinking you don't have a whole lot in common with Gomer. I know. I used to feel the same way!

But I have more in common with Gomer than I might think. In fact we all have something in common with her. We're all prone to wander. We're all tempted to go our own way. We all tend to focus on ourselves and look away from God. In fact the Bible tells us this is true! Hosea 11:7 says, "My people are determined to turn from me."

I know that you've never been married and left your husband. (Neither have I! Yes, I'm married, but I've never left my husband.) But wandering away from God doesn't have to happen on the grand Gomer scale for it to be real and dangerous.

When we look away from God and look to others for approval, we wander.

When we stray from living for Jesus to searching for something that gives us a bigger buzz than God does, we wander.

When our thoughts turn away from God, we begin to wonder who we are. And when we wonder who we are, our actions will start to wander. We'll go away from God to find out who we are. We'll pursue other people and other places to seek out our identity. And that's when we'll find ourselves feeling totally invisible—right in the middle of a major identity crisis.

When we try to figure out who we are away from God, we're never going to know ourselves as God created us to be—amazing, unique, incredible girls of God!

Isn't it a relief to know you're not the only one who struggles with a healthy sense of identity? Isn't it comforting to realize that everyone around you—even the girls who seem so put together and perfect—has had moments when they feel invisible?

As we look at Gomer's life and consider our own, let's think through some important questions. (Again, you can journal your answers or talk about them with your friend, your mom, or a youth leader.)

- What is my identity?
- What is my identity based on?
- Do I identify with my identity?
- Do I accept myself?
- Do I think God accepts me?
- Do I feel invisible?

Finding Your True Identity

There's a "me" in GoMEr—and there's a "you" in Gomer too. It's the part in all of us that is prone to wander away from God. It's the part in all of us that loses our God-given identity—an amazing, unique, incredible girl of God—as we try to find our place in the world. The crazy thing is when we leave God out of the picture, we can't remember who we are!

When we don't accept ourselves, it's hard to believe that God has accepted us. But He has! We can be so quick to see our own weaknesses and flaws. And we can also be quick to overlook all that God sees in us.

God chose you and me as His beloved. And when we, like Gomer, turn away from Him, He is always ready for us to return to Him.

God doesn't focus on *where* we are—stuck in an identity crisis. He focuses on *who* we are. We are never invisible to Him!

Have you been working hard to be accepted? God can free you to accept who you truly are.

Have you spent time wondering who you are? God can show you your real identity—one you can smile at.

Have you felt overlooked, inadequate, or invisible? God can show you once and for all that how you feel is not who you are!

Oh, girl, are you ready to come with me on this journey? Together we can get to a place where how you feel won't define who you are. What you've done in the past won't influence what you can do in the future. Who the media says you should be won't be as strong as who God says you already are! #epicfaith

Instead of constantly striving for acceptance, you'll be free to accept the amazing *you* that God accepts (braces, pimples, and all). Instead of staying stuck in an identity crisis, you'll discover your unimaginable worth. Instead of feeling overlooked or underappreciated, you'll discover that you have never, ever—no not ever—been invisible to God.

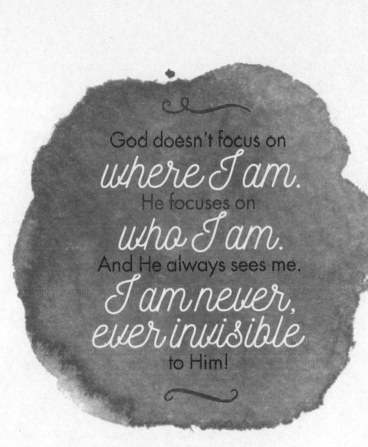

God doesn't focus on
where I am.
He focuses on
who I am.
And He always sees me.
I am never,
ever invisible
to Him!

#TheInvisibleBook

#somebody

What's the price of two or three pet canaries?
Some loose change, right? But God never
overlooks a single one. And he pays even
greater attention to you, down to the last
detail—even numbering the hairs on your
head! So don't be intimidated by all this bully
talk. You're worth more than a million canaries.

—LUKE 12:6-7 MSG

"Are you one of the ballerinas?" asked a little girl. She was no more than four and dressed from head to toe as a princess as she looked up expectantly at Morgan.

"Oh, no," Morgan replied, "I'm not anybody. My sister is in the ballet, and I'm just helping sell refreshments. Would you like a cupcake or maybe a chocolate-chip cookie?"

Disappointment momentarily flickered across the little girl's face before she grinned and announced, "I'll have a cupcake, please!"

Morgan handed the little girl the pink-frosted treat, then turned her attention to the woman next in line. "May I help you?"

"Yes, I'd like a bottle of water and a brownie, please. Did I see you performing earlier today in the matinee?"

"No, that must have been my sister. I'm nobody," Morgan said, turning to pull an ice-cold bottle of water out of the cooler.

Morgan loved serving people at the refreshments table. Sure, it was a volunteer job and she didn't get paid, but it did help raise money for her sister's ballet studio, and Morgan was also able to earn community service hours for school. Best of all, it was fun! Morgan hoped to own a bakery one day, and she'd spent hours at home baking and decorating pastel frosted cupcakes. She also loved this part—chatting with the customers and recommending treats.

The only part she didn't like was the constant questioning. *Who are you? Did you dance in the matinee? Are you part of the ballet school?* Time after time, she patiently smiled and answered, "I'm nobody. I'm not anyone. I'm just working the refreshments table."

By the end of the evening, Morgan was feeling down on herself. Why hadn't she liked ballet when she'd tried it years ago? If she'd stuck with it, she could have been like her sister and her friends with all eyes in the audience focused on them. She could have been the center of attention after the show with little girls crowding around her to touch her glittery costume and tell her how pretty she looked. Sure, her cupcakes had sold out, but compared to her sister, Morgan felt like a nobody.

·~~~~~·

But Morgan wasn't a nobody. *Nobody is a nobody!* Nobody is *just* a refreshments seller—or *just* a student or *just* a sister or *just* a...anything!

When we're doing a behind-the-scenes job that doesn't put us in the spotlight, or even if we're onstage but aren't the star, it can be easy to feel like we don't matter. It can be hard to see our own value when we feel constantly overlooked. It's impossible to feel important when we think what we're doing isn't essential.

Another "nobody" trap we can fall into is associating our value with our virtue. You know, if we are good, we are worthy of being noticed. If we do things perfectly, we will get attention.

I have a feeling that our girl Gomer might have felt that way. After all, if she'd been asked, "Tell me, who are you?" she'd probably have said, "Oh, I'm nobody."

But her answer should have been, "I'm somebody! I'm Gomer! I'm a beloved wife!" Just like Morgan's answer should have been, "I'm somebody! I'm a talented cupcake baker and decorator! I'm a fantastic salesperson! I'm Morgan!"

Longing for Acceptance

The Bible doesn't tell us a lot about Gomer's life, but it tells enough for us to figure out she had a pretty rough childhood. She lived in the Northern Kingdom of Israel a long time ago—way back in the mid-800s BC. (And no, I didn't know her personally. Not even I am that old!) Sure, things were different back then, but people have also been the same throughout time. Young girls have always needed the godly guidance and good example of their parents, and these are two things Gomer most definitely did *not* have growing up.

We don't know tons about Gomer's dad, but we do know that his name, Diblaim, implied that he was not a good father. Back in Bible times, names described a person's character. And Diblaim chose to live in a way that did not honor his marriage commitment to his wife. He lusted after other women, which sent a message to his daughter, Gomer, that she was only a *somebody* if she could attract the attention of guys.

Newsflash! This is the *worst* lesson a father can teach his daughter!

I'm sure Gomer grew up confused about how to relate to men, but she just went with what her father had been showing her. And she became quite a mess. She started to party and go for the wrong kind of guy—any guy who would give her attention solely based on the way she dressed, the type of makeup she wore, and how she styled her hair. She wasn't the kind of girl that guys took seriously. You know what I mean. In fact there were even whispers around Israel that Gomer was actually a prostitute.

I imagine that while she thought she looked good on the outside, Gomer probably didn't feel good about herself on the inside. She was stuck in painful self-awareness, lost in insecurity, and longing to be accepted for who she was inside—not how she was seen on the outside. Of course, I'm using my imagination here based on a few facts from Scripture. All we really know about Gomer's family is the name of her dad and the way she lived as an adult. But it makes sense.

> God accepts me for who I am on the inside
> no matter what I look like on the outside.

What about Gomer's mom? The Bible doesn't say anything about her, but I think she was probably one of those mothers who acted like nothing inappropriate was going on in her family. I'm guessing she made excuses for her husband's behavior and didn't teach her daughter right from wrong. She didn't show Gomer that she was *somebody*. She didn't tell her that God loved her and that His love was more than enough to give her value.

Overlooked and undervalued, Gomer felt unworthy—like a complete and total nobody.

Now, here's where the story gets really interesting. Even though Gomer saw herself as invisible and least likely to stand out in a good way, Hosea saw her. And he chose her. What happened next is almost like a Disney princess fairy tale...only better!

Who? Me?

It's super hard to imagine a guy like Hosea—a preacher, a man of God—marrying a girl like Gomer. That just doesn't happen! Why would an eligible bachelor like him choose someone like her when he could have his pick of all the godly girls in Israel?

And what's even more bizarre was that Hosea didn't date—ever! Unlike Gomer, who was hanging out with guy after guy, Hosea was busy doing his work as a prophet. I'm guessing nobody even expected him to get married! And if they did think about him getting married, it was to a sweet, piano playing, Bible studying young woman. You know, a good girl with good grades from a good family—basically the perfect Christian girl! But *Gomer* was the girl God chose for Hosea.

Just imagine all the gossip surrounding their relationship. And then when Hosea announced that God had told him to marry Gomer—wait...*what?*

I'm guessing Gomer herself couldn't quite believe it either. *Me? Marry him? Is this for real? How can this guy really love me this much? He knows who I am, doesn't he? He knows I don't have the best reputation. He knows what people are saying about me. What on earth is he thinking?*

All Gomer could do was say yes. How could she turn down the love of such a great guy—especially when Hosea told her that God wanted him to marry her? (I suspect that Gomer probably heard God's voice too!)

The rumor mill must have exploded when their engagement was announced! *Can you believe it? Has Hosea totally lost his mind? She's not good enough for him! He deserves better! Of all the good, pure, lovely girls he could have chosen, why did he pick her?*

The gossip continued to fly after the couple said their wedding vows. One big question was on the lips of everyone at the reception. Why would *he* marry *her*?

And that's the same thing I'm asking myself centuries later as I read the book of Hosea in my Bible. *Why did a guy like Hosea marry a girl like Gomer?*

Do you know why I'm asking myself this question? It's because deep down I believe that Gomer is not good enough for Hosea. You probably know some unlikely couples and ask the questions: Why is he dating her? She flirts with every guy around when he's not looking! Or: What's a sweet girl like her doing with an arrogant jerk like him?

Gomer is dirty. Hosea is clean.

She's full of flaws. He's fabulous.

She can't be trusted. He's too trusting.

She's a nobody. He's a somebody.

She doesn't deserve his attention—or his love.

How would you feel if you were there in the church on Gomer and Hosea's wedding day? Would you feel that a messed-up girl like Gomer deserved to marry a put-together guy like Hosea?

Now, think about God and His overwhelming love for you.

Jesus said, "God never overlooks a single [canary]. And he pays even greater attention to you, down to the last detail—even numbering the hairs on your head!" (Luke 12:6-7 MSG).

Here's the deal: God never overlooks you! He chose you, and He loves you.

Why does God love you with such an amazing yet simple love?

Why does He accept the imperfect you? After all, compared to His purity, you're dirty. We *all* are.

So what is God's love for you based on? Why in the world does He choose you, accept you, and love you?

Scandalous Love

You can bet that Hosea's love for Gomer created a stir around Israel. It was simply scandalous that a prophet would court and then marry a woman with her reputation. What did that say about Hosea—that he would marry a girl like Gomer?

If Hosea's love for Gomer is a picture of God's love for us, what does that say about God? What does that say about us? And how did this scandalous love ever happen in the first place anyway?

John 15:16 says, "You did not choose me, but I chose you."

God's "just because" kind of love is not a love you earn for being especially loyal or lovely. It's much simpler than that. He loves us with the same kind of love Hosea loved Gomer with—a "no matter what" love that is so simple that it's sometimes hard to understand.

God chose to love you.

That's it!

Have you ever thought, *How can a pure, perfect God accept me or even love me? I'm not good enough for His love! Isn't He above loving me?*

I've definitely struggled with thoughts like these!

And the more I try to see the *me* in Gomer, the more I have to honestly deal with these questions. Over and over, I see this God—this amazingly patient, passionate God who loves me *no matter what*. To me that is scandalous!

God says He has loved us with an everlasting love (Jeremiah 31:3). It's hard to wrap our mind around the word *everlasting*. Sure, a certain boring class might seem everlasting. The time you have to wait to get your driver's license might seem everlasting. A superbad movie might seem everlasting. But, really, what does it mean that God has chosen to love us with an everlasting love?

Everlasting means that God's love for us never had a starting date. Because He is eternal and has always existed, the same is true of His love. And if He never started to love, girl, He cannot ever stop loving. Crazy, isn't it?

God not only loves you because He chose to, He also loves you because He is love. First John 4:8 states it plain and simple: *God is love.*

> God loves me with a
> no-matter-what kind of love.

God gives us His love because He is love. Nothing forces Him to love us, and nothing will ever stop Him from loving us.

He is love. God's essence is love, so for Him to know you is to love you. Yes, you!

God knows us so well! He knew we would look in the mirror and see all our flaws and imperfections—on the outside as well as on the inside. He knew we would question how an amazing God like Him could love someone so imperfect as us. So He proved it:

> This is how God showed his love among us: He sent his one and only Son into the world that we might live through him. This is love: not that we loved God, but that he loved us and sent his Son as an atoning sacrifice for our sins.
>
> 1 John 4:9-10

Jesus is all the proof you need that God loves you. *You are loved because God is love.* It's that simple. That deep. That profound. That scandalous!

God's love is something we humbly accept by faith. If we reject His love, we reject Him. If we say we're not worthy or deserving of His love, we say He's not worthy of being loved. To say we're not good enough for His love is to say He's not good enough.

Is this starting to make some sense? When you're feeling unloved or invisible, the absolute best thing you can do is simply and humbly receive God's love. Think about it. Say to yourself over and over, *I am loved because God is love.* No matter how you're feeling about yourself, God is always love. And He always loves you.

Whenever we compare ourselves to others—whether in person or online—we can find ourselves slipping into the "not me, not-good-enough" mindset. Did you know that when we think this way, we diminish God's worth? That's not what we mean to do, of course, but that's what we're doing.

God's love is a big deal. It's the biggest deal ever!

Think about this: You are God's beloved daughter. That is the most important—and most true—identity you could ever have.

Can you just take a moment and say that out loud? (If someone is around, I give you permission to whisper it!) *I am loved because God is love.* Good! Now say it again. *I am loved because God is love.*

That was true for Gomer, and it's true for you and me. We are loved because God is love. We are His beloved daughters. You are God's beloved child. That's who is reading this book right now—God's chosen and beloved. Oh, man! I am so honored!

You're Not a Nobody!

When Gomer married Hosea, she stopped being the woman she used to be. Her childhood didn't define her anymore. Her wild years were a thing of the past. Hosea accepted her—the real her, the flawed her.

Gomer became a brand-new woman on her wedding day—radiant, beautiful, pure.

Hosea's love made Gomer lovely.

Just like Gomer, you are loved. God chose you. He loved you while you were still a sinner. Romans 5:8 says, "But God demonstrates his own love for us in this: While we were still sinners, Christ died for us."

Do you hear those amazing words? *While we were still sinners...* God doesn't expect you to become perfect before He gives you the gifts of His attention and His love and also the gift of eternal life. He doesn't love you only after you eliminate all your flaws. The first thing He ever did for you is love you. And after He loves you, you become lovely! Your value comes from God's deep-rooted value.

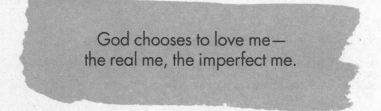

God chooses to love me—
the real me, the imperfect me.

Just like Hosea chose to love Gomer, God chooses to love you—the real you, the imperfect you. God loves the you who failed her math test. God loves the you who got made fun of for wearing the wrong kind of jeans or not knowing the words to the latest song. God loves the you who sometimes yells at her brother, forgets to do her chores, or gossips about a friend.

He will never stop loving you no matter what!

So look into the mirror and see God's love reflected back in your own image. And repeat these words once again: *I am loved because God is love.*

God already loves you, so what you need to do next is agree to see yourself the way God sees you. That's what Gomer did with Hosea's love. She chose to see herself as he saw her. Yet, this can be a really hard thing to do, especially on those days when you feel like you don't measure up or when you feel like a nobody.

Here's something super important to remember: You are not your current failures or your past mistakes. You are also not all the awards you received, the good grades you achieved, or the number of followers on your Instagram.

You are not what you do or what you did.

You are not what you haven't done, what you should have done, or what you wish you'd done.

You are not the hard times you've gone through.

You are not all the bad days you've had.

You are not the rumors someone else has spread about you.

You are not a nobody!

You are a chosen, loved daughter of the King whom God calls His beloved. Since God Himself is King of the universe, girl, that makes you a princess!

You are His beloved daughter, and that's who God sees when He looks at you. Can you begin to accept the you whom God sees? Go ahead and crown yourself with a tiara. It's totally fitting for a daughter of the King!

Okay, here's an assignment for you to do right now. Yes, I can hear you groaning! *More homework?! I already have enough of that! I'm totally drowning in tests and quizzes!* Don't worry. This assignment is quick, easy, and fun!

Grab a colorful pen and write down the following statements on some bright Post-it notes and stick them everywhere! Or find some cheap lipstick and use it to write these truths on your bathroom mirror. Come on, I dare you! Then read them over and over to yourself so you can start identifying with the *you* God sees:

- God loves me and His love makes me lovely.
- I am loved because God is love.
- I am not the be-tolerated; I am the beloved!

Yes! You are God's beloved, and so am I. So is your BFF. So are your sister and your mom. So is the girl who got the part in the play that you wanted. And so is the girl who sits by herself every day at lunch. We are all deeply loved by God.

Let's all try to trust God more with our feelings when it comes to this, okay? You're not always going to feel loved or accepted, but how you feel does not define who you are. You are not your feelings!

You may feel invisible, but you are not. You are seen and loved.

So when you start feeling like a nobody—rejected, unaccepted, or like you don't matter at all—remember that your feelings are not going to give you the final say on this matter. You need to trust God's opinion on this one, not your own.

When your feelings start taking over, grab those Post-it notes or look at the words written in lipstick on your bathroom mirror. And say those three truths over and over again. Say them so often that if someone says to you, "Tell me who you are," you'll totally forget to say your name as you shout out, "God's love makes me lovely!" and "I am loved because God is love!" and "I am not the be-tolerated, I am the beloved!"

Sure, it sounds incredibly silly, but trust me, it works!

You'll no longer see yourself as the sister of the ballerina at the beginning of this chapter saw herself—a nobody, someone whose work and talents were of no value, just another unimportant face in the crowd. You'll instead see yourself as somebody—God's lovely somebody.

Nice to meet you, you lovely thing!

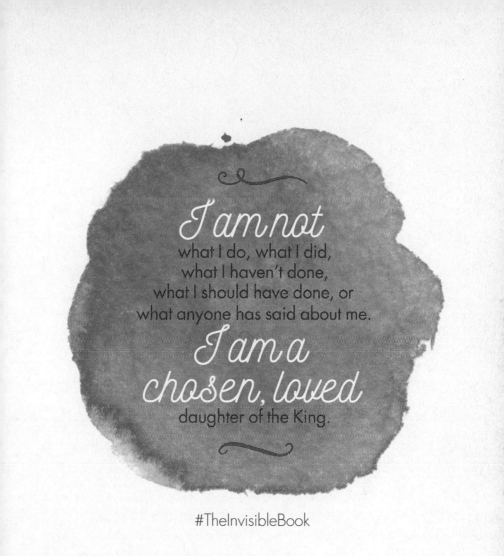

I am not
what I do, what I did,
what I haven't done,
what I should have done, or
what anyone has said about me.

**I am a
chosen, loved**
daughter of the King.

#TheInvisibleBook

#gorgeous

*Now we look inside, and what we see
is that anyone united with the Messiah
gets a fresh start, is created new. The
old life is gone; a new life burgeons!*
—2 CORINTHIANS 5:17 MSG

Justine yanked the third of three plastic storage bins out of the closet, then opened up the first one, and began to sort through the summer clothes inside. She held up the first tank top. Wow! It looked so tiny! She knew she'd had a huge growth spurt this past year, but she didn't realize she'd grown *that* much. Same story with the next tank top and the next.

After tossing most of the tank tops into a hand-me-down pile, Justine tried on a few that looked like they might fit. Nope, too small. Too tight. Her body had changed, and it looked like her wardrobe might need to change too.

Maybe the sundresses still fit, Justine hoped. Same story—too short, too tight. Into the hand-me-down pile went a stack of brightly colored sundresses. *I love these*, Justine thought with regret.

Shorts? Same story! The shorts no longer fit her changing body. And swimsuits? Forget it! *Looks like the only things that still fit are my flip-flops and sunglasses,* Justine said to herself with a sigh. *Good thing the flip-flops were a little too big last summer!*

"Mom!" Justine called down the stairs. "We need to go shopping for summer clothes! I outgrew my whole wardrobe!"

·~~~~~·

Have you ever had an experience like Justine's? After what seems like the longest winter ever, you're super ready for shorts and T-shirts and sundresses and flip-flops. But something has happened! Your body has changed. You've had a growth spurt or gained weight or lost weight! You might be in the best shape of your life, but your old clothes no longer fit. You need a whole new wardrobe. (If you love to shop, this sounds awesome! If you're not into shopping, it's pure torture!)

You're ready to pass on your old things and fill your closet with new stuff. There's even a Bible verse that's fitting for this situation. "If any man be in Christ, he is a new creature: old things are passed away; behold, all things are become new" (2 Corinthians 5:17 KJV).

Okay, okay, this verse isn't really about outgrowing last year's summer clothes and hitting the mall, but it's still a good picture. After we experience this kind of a change, our old clothes don't fit us anymore. They feel uncomfortable, and they look terrible.

It's like that with your old life—the way you lived before you knew Jesus. Now that you're a Christian, suddenly the old ways are uncomfortable. It's no longer fun to talk about people behind their backs. You feel bad for yelling at your sister. You realize that your current group of friends—even if they're thought of as popular— make a lot of poor choices.

When you are in Christ—when you're clothed in His righteousness—you're made new. You're adorned in the most recent fashion, wearing the latest style—Jesus' love and forgiveness. And the *new* you is the *true* you.

When you have Jesus in your life, you look different. Your new identity flatters the real you, and others are going to wonder where you got such great style.

Gomer experienced the same thing when all was made new in her life. When Hosea married her, it changed who she was. She was able to leave her old life in the past, and she became Gomer—beloved bride, chosen wife—just like in a fairy tale.

Since our new identity in Christ is our true identity, we want to live like it, don't we? So how do you do that? How do you pack up who you were in the past and put it in the hand-me-down pile?

Wear Your New Wardrobe

When we first say yes to Jesus—just like Gomer said yes to Hosea—it seems so easy to pack away our past and start living for God. We get involved in a small group Bible study. We order a cute new devotional from Amazon. We start writing in a prayer journal. We invite our friends to youth group. We copy our favorite Bible verses onto colorful index cards and post them all around our bedroom.

All it takes, though, is just one bad day to send us back to living the way we did and believing the old lies: *I'm not good enough. I'm not worthy of His love. He couldn't really love someone like me.*

It's like reaching into the hand-me-down bag for just one thing to wear just one more time. Before we know it, our closet is full of things we fished out of the hand-me-down bag—those items we promised ourselves we'd wear just one last time.

But we don't need to be wearing hand-me-downs anymore when

we can be wearing fashionable, brand-new things! Because God chose you and loves you, that frees you to live as the true *you*. You don't need to keep living in the past anymore. In fact, in order to not dwell *in* your past, you can't dwell *on* your past. That was then. This is now!

Isaiah 43:18-19 says, "Forget the former things; do not dwell on the past. See, I am doing a new thing! Now it springs up; do you not perceive it?" Girl, I want to wear my new clothes! I want to live life to the fullest, confident of who I am in Christ. I know you want to live like this too.

But our feelings get in the way. Our feelings are incredibly powerful, and they have such loud voices: *You aren't really loved—you're just tolerated! You'll only be accepted by God if your behavior is perfectly acceptable to Him! There's nothing new and amazing about you—you're the same old loser you've always been!*

Those feelings can yank us right out of the present truth of our new identity in Christ and throw us straight into the hand-me-down pile of an identity crisis.

So how do you keep this from happening? How do you tune out the emotions and thoughts that make you feel bad about yourself? You focus on three transforming truths, powerful statements backed up by powerful Scriptures. Tell yourself these truths over and over to help live the way God wants you to live—as a positive, confident girl of God.

Three Transforming Truths

Are you ready for these three truth statements? Grab a pen and write them down so you can look at them and repeat them anytime and as often as you need them. Here they are.

Transforming Truth #1: I am dearly loved.

Colossians 3:12 says, "Therefore, as God's chosen people, holy and dearly loved, clothe yourselves with compassion, kindness, humility, gentleness and patience."

Gomer was dearly loved. I am dearly loved. You are dearly loved. This is real and true—and it's what you need to tell yourself every single day.

Speaking of telling things to yourself, did you know that there's a certain way you should speak to yourself? I once read a study (which was published in the *Journal of Personality and Social Psychology**, so you know it's legit) that said the best way to talk to yourself is in the second-person "you" or in the third person.

Wait, you say that you don't talk to yourself? Sure you do! (It's okay if you don't admit it, though.) Let me give you an example. Let's say you're about to take a super hard test. Instead of saying, "I can do this!" tell yourself, "You can do this!" or "[insert your name here] can do this!" It does sound a little funny, like when I walk around telling myself, "Jennifer is capable!" But it's proven to work.

The study looked at two groups of people—one group that used the first-person "I" pronoun to talk to themselves (like we normally do) and another group that used the second-person "you" and third-person own-name pronouns. The people who called themselves "you" and their own names not only *felt* more positive about them-selves at the end of the study, but they also *performed* better. They felt less hesitant about their abilities and more confident about their actions.

What's the lesson here? I should walk around making statements

---

* Ethan Kross, et al., "Self-Talk as a Regulatory Mechanism: How You Do It Matters," *Journal of Personality and Social Psychology* 106, no. 2 (2014: 304-24).

like "Jennifer is loved" or "You are loved" rather than saying, "I am loved." Changing a few little words can make a huge difference!

So, feel free to talk to yourself anytime. And when you do, tell yourself the truth in the best possible way—a proven way that will get through to your heart and mind and reassure you that you're a *somebody* who matters. You're worth something!

Transforming Truth #2: I am accepted.

God backs up this truth in His Word: "...to the praise of the glory of His grace, by which He made us accepted in the Beloved" (Ephesians 1:6 NKJV).

Just like the total surprise of Gomer being accepted by Hosea, we—with all our flaws and imperfections and mess-ups—are accepted by a perfect God.

Amazing, isn't it? You're not only accepted *in* the beloved, you're accepted *by* the beloved Himself—God. You have value! You have worth! You are visible to God!

When you accepted Christ, He accepted you. Sure, you'll have your moments when you feel rejected. That's perfectly normal! But remember how you feel is not who you are. You are accepted—no exception! So find a mirror right now, look straight into your own eyes, and repeat these words, "You are accepted!"

How I feel is not who I am.
I am accepted by Christ
even with all my imperfections!

Transforming Truth #3: I am complete.

Colossians 2:10 (NKJV) says, "You are complete in Him, who is the head of all principality and power."

When you give your life to Jesus, you become complete in Him. This means that there's nothing you need to do to earn His love or your salvation. His grace—His perfect love—has made you complete. When you have Jesus in your life, you have no need for anything more.

It's like having a complete breakfast instead of grabbing a few Pop-Tarts on the way out the door. When you eat a complete breakfast—scrambled eggs, bacon, toast, a fruit smoothie—you don't need anything else. All your nutritional needs have been met. When you eat the Pop-Tarts, you might *think* you've had a complete breakfast (hey, it *was* food and you *were* in a hurry!), but your body will soon let you know that a meal of Pop-Tarts is not the best way to start your day.

When we have Christ, we don't need anything else. Yes, you can sometimes feel like you want something else—remember how your feelings work!—but discontentment is a *feeling*, not your *reality*. When you have Christ in your life, you have everything. He makes you whole.

Everyone loves a good fairy tale, right? When you become a Christian, you are instantly—*poof*—made spiritually whole. It's just like a fairy godmother waves her wand to turn tattered rags into a gorgeous gown. The change is instantaneous when you open your heart to Christ. The stunning goodness of Jesus fills your heart and your life.

When Jesus died on the cross for our sins, His final words were, "It is finished." And when He said it, He meant it!

It is finished. You are complete. So look in the mirror right now, girl, and speak that truth to yourself, "[Your name], you are complete!"

Mirror, Mirror

Now, girl, please notice something here. When you speak these three transforming truths to yourself in the order I gave them to you, you say, "I am *loved*. I am *accepted*. I am *complete*." Look at the first letter of each of those three words. L-A-C. They make a word—well, a misspelled word, but it's still a word! (Don't tell your English teacher, please!) It's a word you can remember. *Lac*. And even though it's spelled wrong, the message is totally right. You and I *lack* nothing in Christ. In Him we are new creations—loved, accepted, and complete.

Now, I know you've used a mirror a few times. You might have a full-length mirror mounted in your room so you can check your whole outfit before heading off to school or going shopping with your friends. Maybe you use a makeup mirror, or maybe you just snap a pic of yourself with your iPhone to see yourself. And I'm sure you have a mirror in your bathroom that you use when you brush your teeth, wash your face, and do your hair.

Did you know that you have another kind of mirror too? You probably have one in your room, and you might not even know it's a mirror! God's Word is a mirror that reflects the truth of who you are—the visible, lovely you who is God's beloved daughter. So if you have a Bible, you have the most flattering mirror ever!

The Bible is a perfect mirror that reflects the truth of who I am.

Did you know that mirrors are imperfect? What they reflect is close to what you look like but not quite. The mirrors in your home and at the stores are flawed, and they make your image ever-so-slightly distorted. The Bible, though, is a perfect mirror. It's the only mirror you can look into and see 100 percent truth.

If you looked into your bathroom mirror this morning and saw a streak of toothpaste smeared across your cheek or mascara smudges on your eyelids, you wouldn't leave your bathroom before wiping them off, would you? You wouldn't just walk away from the mirror and forget what you looked like. That would be ridiculous!

It's easy, though, to forget what we see when we look into the mirror of God's Word. When we do that, it's like walking away and continuing to live our lives with toothpaste on our cheeks or mascara on our eyelids. If we forget what we look like through the eyes of Jesus, it can have a major effect on how we see ourselves and what we think of ourselves.

James 1:23-24 says, "Anyone who listens to the word but does not do what it says is like someone who looks at his face in a mirror and, after looking at himself, goes away and immediately forgets what he looks like." What James is saying is that when we hear something but don't do anything about it—refusing to change the way we think, act, or even pray—we're like that person who looks in the mirror and does nothing about the toothpaste or mascara.

And it's not just our sins, flaws, or imperfections we see in the mirror. God's Word also shows us truth and beauty—like the amazingness of being totally loved, unconditionally accepted, and 100 percent complete in Jesus!

Isn't that exciting to know? When you look into the mirror of God's Word, you'll see everything that is true! And your image is going to look incredible. You'll see exactly what you look like in

God's eyes—a beloved, accepted, and complete girl of God. You look gorgeous!

I'm going to give you one teeny-weeny caution here, though. The point of looking in a mirror is *not* to find yourself or admire yourself or obsess about how incredibly important you are. The point of looking in the mirror is to see God and understand that you are found in Him.

When you look into the mirror of God's Word, you see the true image of God. And that gives you a right view of yourself. You'll see two sides—your flawed humanness as well as your incredible value as a girl made right by God. Cool, huh?

Even if mirrors make you nervous—even if you're worried you'll see acne or crooked teeth or a nose you don't exactly love—be sure to look into the mirror of truth every morning (and every afternoon and evening while you're at it!) to see who you really are. And then get out there and start living what you're learning! I like to say, "Practice what you perceive." That means you need to start believing you are the amazing girl God created and living like the great girl you are!

So let's not just hear what God is telling us, even though that's super important too. Let's take the next step and *do*. Let's say "I do" every time we gaze into the mirror of God's Word.

I do believe the truth that I'm loved.

I do agree with the truth that I'm accepted.

I do trust the truth that I'm complete in Christ.

Christ has changed you so much for the better! He's given you a whole new wardrobe brimming with confidence and grace. So get rid of those hand-me-downs and put on your brand-new clothes. After all, God has given you a whole new identity. You're spiritually whole, lovely, valuable, stunning—totally gorgeous inside and out!

#thoughts

So if you're serious about living this new resurrection life with Christ, act like it. Pursue the things over which Christ presides. Don't shuffle along, eyes to the ground, absorbed with the things right in front of you. Look up, and be alert to what is going on around Christ—that's where the action is. See things from his perspective.

—COLOSSIANS 3:1-2 MSG

Sophia thought glumly, *Same old Monday.* She'd just had a week off from school for spring break, but she might as well have just stayed in school. It would have been more exciting! Sure, it was great to sleep in, but while her friends were vacationing in Florida or working at church camp, she'd been stuck at home babysitting her annoying brothers. She'd been keeping up with her friends on Instagram, and the photos they'd shared of themselves—sunbathing in Destin or playing games with a bunch of cute little kids at the church camp—just proved that she was missing out on absolutely everything.

Nothing exciting ever happens to me! Sophia told herself. Looking at her planner, she saw the proof of her unexciting week right there on paper: school, babysit, study, and repeat. Even going to the movies or the mall was getting a little boring. She wanted to do something different, something adventurous. Climb a mountain! Visit another country! Take art or dance classes!

Oh, well, she said to herself with a sigh, *just another few weeks until soccer starts again. Then, finally, I'll have something new to break up my totally boring routine. And I guess there's the youth retreat next month. That should be fun too, but it seems so far away right now.* Heading for the couch, she grabbed the remote to see what was on TV and thought, *Probably a rerun—just like my same old boring life!*

·~~~·

We've all had days like Sophia's. We feel like everyone else is out living an exciting life and we're stuck at home watching the same old shows. Facebook and Twitter can make us feel even worse. In fact you've probably heard the term FOMO—fear of missing out. We feel like we're missing out on everything and stuck in the same old routine while everyone else is having the time of their life.

When Gomer first got together with Hosea, her social media would have looked pretty enviable. She sure wasn't missing out! If I were to tweet out their strange love story or reduce it to a series of Facebook posts, this is how it might read:

> Spiritual guy pursues scandalous girl
> #unbelievable
> Sincere guy dates sketchy girl
> #ishecrazy

God-centered guy marries self-centered girl
#luckygirl
Devalued daughter becomes highly-valued bride
#beautiful
Aimless woman becomes chosen wife
#amazinggrace

What a story! What a life adventure! What a change! In spite of the odds, Gomer is no longer the invisible girl. She's now the chosen, loved Mrs. Hosea. Could her new life look any more different from her previous life? I don't think so! Gomer's new life was dreamy, and her marriage was just like a fairy tale. What could possibly go wrong?

Um, can you say everything?

We might assume that this romance was headed for "happily ever after" right after the wedding, but that's not what happened. Yes, the wedding was beautiful, and the honeymoon incredible, but then came the marriage. It's like any situation—new school, new sport, new youth group. At first everything is fresh and exciting. There are all those crisp new school supplies and clothes, never-been-worn swimsuits or gymnastics leotards, new friends to make, and lessons to learn. But somewhere along the way, things become routine. Some of your classes are hard—really hard! You get injured and have to take a few weeks off from your favorite sport. Some of the kids in youth group are acting kind of cliquey, and it seems like they're leaving you out. *Can I just go back to summer vacation?* you think to yourself.

So much for everything being new and exciting!

Gomer's new life starts out the same way as a new school year. She's never felt so secure, so happy. Her new little house is so cozy! Cooking dinner every night is just plain fun. And she loves to surprise Hosea on Saturdays and come up with outings for just the two of them—picnics, hikes, and romantic dinners out. She's always so happy to see him when he gets home from work and makes sure she hugs him as soon as he walks through the door. Yes, her new life is like a Disney princess's on steroids!

Gradually, though, there's a shift. She gets a little bored with making dinner every night and substitutes takeout for a few meals. *It's only a few times a week*, she tells herself.

She skips her early morning women's Bible study to sleep in. *I'm so tired. I really need the rest. I can go next week*, she thinks.

She stops arranging the fun outings and adventures. *Why should I always be the one to plan our weekends? Hosea never plans anything! Anyway, hanging out at home costs less money.*

Soon Gomer finds out the reason she's been feeling so lethargic. She's about to become a mom! And with this news, she's relieved to know the fairy tale isn't fading. It's merely changing. At least she hopes that's the case!

Gomer is excited to become a mom. She's determined to be a better mother to her child than her own mother was to her. Better yet, she's super thankful to have a guy like Hosea as the father of her child. Her own dad was about the worst dad a girl could ever have. And Hosea? He's perfect! Even his name means "salvation"!

Gomer knows Hosea is the ideal guy to lead their little family. After all, he saved *her*—saved her from her past, saved her from her insecurity, saved her from feeling freaked out about her future.

Soon the happy day arrives. It's a boy! The proud parents name their new son Jezreel, which means "God scatters" (Hosea 1:4). Okay, you probably don't know many guys named *Jezreel*, and just wait until you find out the name of Gomer and Hosea's next kid! But what's important to remember here is that the names of Gomer and Hosea's children were part of God's message to His people the Israelites.

God told Hosea to name their firstborn Jezreel to show that He was going to put an end to the leadership of the house of Israel. I wonder what the happy new momma Gomer thought of that? That's a pretty big name—and a pretty intense message—for such a little guy!

Soon baby Jezreel was off and crawling, making messes and getting into everything. Before long he could use a sippy cup and was well on his way to becoming a big boy...and a big brother. Toddler Jezreel now had a new baby sister!

Are you ready for little sister's name? (Remember, I told you it was an interesting one!) Gomer and Hosea named their sweet baby girl Lo-Ruhamah (Hosea 1:6), which meant "not pitied." What a name!

Now, little Lo-Ruhamah's proud daddy was also a pretty smart prophet, so he realized right away what God was telling His people through his baby girl's name. The Israelites had been refusing to listen to God, and He was no longer going to have compassion on them. That may sound pretty harsh, but God always does what's best for His people!

Getting back to Gomer, though, this former party girl was now home all day taking care of a baby and a toddler. If you've ever babysat kids those ages, you know how exhausting they can be—even if they are supercute!

As Gomer changed diaper after diaper and swayed her little ones to sleep in the rocking chair, she found herself daydreaming about how exciting her life used to be—before every day was filled with the same thing. And then guess what happened? Yep, you got it! Baby number three was on the way!

Jezreel and Lo-Ruhamah now had a baby brother, who his parents named Lo-Ammi or "not my people" (Hosea 1:9). This one sounds pretty harsh too, doesn't it? His name was a message to the

Israelites that God's tolerance for their sinful actions was eventually going to run out, and when it did, He would no longer call Israel His own.

Same Old, Same Old

Tough stuff, isn't it? Back in the day, though, it was totally normal for God to communicate His message through names. Gomer was a mom. Hosea was a dad. They loved their little children, and God loved them too. Their names didn't mean that God was going to walk away from them or that He loved them any less. They were just part of the message God was communicating to His people through Hosea His prophet. (Remember Hosea's job? The whole family was involved!)

Yep, with three young children to care for, Gomer's life had completely changed. She was busier than she'd ever been *and* more exhausted. It was all she could do to throw dinner together every night. In fact, fish sticks with macaroni and cheese were pretty typical meals in Gomer's house!

And forget about dressing up. Why bother when she did the same old thing day after day? Gomer used to dress like a model, but her regular uniform these days was a food-stained, frumpy old T-shirt and a pair of mom jeans. (You know how it is when you're studying for finals or writing a big paper—a baggy tee and pajama pants count as getting dressed, am I right?)

Lip gloss? Forget that! She couldn't even find a tube—even if she'd had the time to apply it. Forever picking up toys, she had zero energy for putting on makeup. At the end of the day, she was grateful to grab one of Hosea's oversized T-shirts, throw it on, and fall exhausted into bed. So much for the party girl with the exciting life!

But let's look at the reality here. Gomer was bored! It's not that she no longer loved her husband or kids. It's just that sometimes when you're stuck doing the same old thing, it seems like everyone else is having way more fun. Everyone else is busy doing stuff that makes them look like *somebody* (especially when you see all those Instagram pictures). In comparison you feel like a nobody. That's what happened to Gomer. She felt like she was right back to being an overlooked, unimportant, invisible nobody.

You can relate, right? You know what it's like to feel swallowed up by the dailiness of your life—doing the same old chores, attending the same old classes, working on the same old homework, seeing the same old faces in the hallway over and over again. You have a good life, and you know you should be thankful for it, but it's just so easy to feel invisible in the middle of it.

I have a term for this: *familiarity fatigue.* When you feel this way, you just want to do something different or be someone different! Maybe you're counting down the years or months or days until you graduate. Perhaps you're just feeling stuck where you're at. You want to make new friends, have new experiences, and see new places.

That's totally normal!

Sometimes it can be super reassuring to hang out in a familiar space, say on a rainy Saturday when you and your BFF are sprawled out on your floor watching YouTube while chocolate-chip cookies bake in the oven.

Other times you feel hopelessly stuck. Instagram shows you pictures of friends on vacation hanging out together or playing a sport you wish you played. You look at your own life and start thinking, *This isn't good enough. I want something more.*

Stop! I'm going to warn you right now that those feelings put you in the danger zone. When you're looking for a door to escape—especially when it's a result of comparing yourself to others—there's a good chance it's going to lead you away from God and into the land of self.

That's when you need to think about what you're thinking about!

Thought Trouble

Just like Gomer we live out our new and true identity in the dailiness of life. We—the chosen, beloved girls of God—are surrounded by papers to write, tests to study for, group projects to finish, practices to attend, siblings to babysit, messy rooms to clean, chores to do, friendships to develop, social media to stay current with, and don't forget about reading the Bible and going to youth group activities. That's life as a busy teen girl!

It may be a terrific life, but sometimes *where* we are distracts us from the amazingness of *who* we are. And sometimes like Gomer, we can become so familiar with the incredible truth that God loves us that the miracle loses its luster.

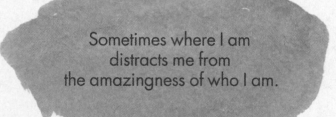

Sometimes where I am
distracts me from
the amazingness of who I am.

That's when we begin to feel invisible. We forget what God thinks about us, and we start feeling like we no longer matter to anyone. That's when the questions of self-doubt begin. *Am I good enough? Who am I, anyway? Does anyone even notice me? Does anyone think I'm pretty? Why can't I ever do anything right? Is this really all there is? I wonder what it would be like if...* When our minds turn to questions like these, it's tempting to start out on a new, unknown path. And as we focus on who we are in school or what our friends think of us—as we focus on who we are in this right-here, right-now world—it's easy to become overly self-aware and eventually self-absorbed.

I need to do more with my life than this, we think. *Why does everyone else seem to have more friends than I do?* we wonder. *I need more to make myself happy*, we decide.

Suddenly you're no longer stuck in a rut. You're stuck in insecurity!

Your situation hasn't changed. You're still the same person doing the same things. What *has* changed is your thinking.

Corrupt Versus Correct Thinking

When we wander from God, we automatically trade in correct thinking for corrupt thinking. Right for wrong.

Correct thinking says, *I'm a beloved girl of God. He loves me, and His love makes me holy. God sees me and knows who I am.*

Corrupt thinking quickly responds, *Well, I sure don't feel very beloved! God could never love me completely. After all, I'm not so lovely or lovable. What I am is invisible! It's time for me to go find out who I really am.*

But you just *have* to trust that God loves you because He is love. That's truth! And when you forget the truth of who God is, you'll eventually reject the truth of who you are.

You bet there will be days when you feel unworthy, unseen, unacceptable—oh, just let me say it—like the ultimate loser! (At least I have those days!) We all have those moments when we focus less on who we are in Jesus and more on how we feel about ourselves. And the longer we neglect the truth, the sooner we'll just flat-out reject the truth.

That's what Gomer did. That's what people have done since the beginning of time!

Truth and Temptation

While stay-at-home mom Gomer drooped on her couch and daydreamed about how adorable her clothes once were, how handsome guys once flirted with her, and how much she missed the buzz of going out every night, her thoughts went wandering from the truth of who she was to the temptation of who she wanted to be.

Does that sound familiar? We've all wanted to be someone else—a pop star, a fashion model, the most popular girl at school, the best athlete, and the girl with the cutest clothes (and let's add in *car* and *guy* while we're at it!).

When we're thinking about who we wish we were, we're ignoring the truth of who we actually are—the amazing girl God created us to be—and giving in to the temptation of wanting to be someone else. We forget about our completeness in Christ and accept the lie that what we are is not enough. Slowly but surely we trade the truth for deception—and for temptation.

When I stalked Facebook that day I road tripped, I was wondering how I could "become as popular as she was" or "feel better about who I was" or "be noticed by more people." I was trading in correct thinking about who I was in Christ for corrupt thinking about who I was *not* according to this world.

How I think eventually becomes what I do.

Oh, sweet girl, beware of neglecting the truth of who you are because it will lead you to rejecting the truth of who you are.

You are too valuable to God to let corrupt thinking confuse you about your identity. How you think eventually becomes what you do. Thoughts lead to actions. So before we follow Gomer into the next scene of her story, let's pause and think about our own stories. Let's ask ourselves some important questions:

- How can I choose correct thinking over corrupt thinking?
- What can I do to see the amazing in the everyday?
- How can I trust that God sees me even when I feel invisible?

Phroneo

Are you studying a foreign language? If you are, then you'll pick up on this concept pretty quickly! Not yet? There's no time like the present to learn!

I'm going to teach you one Greek word: *phroneo*. When you *phroneo* (yes, it's a verb!), you "set your affection on things above, not on things on the earth" (Colossians 3:2 KJV). So what does "setting your affection" mean? Think of the verb *set* as referring to cement. It dries, slowly hardens, and becomes *set*.

When you do this, you slowly but surely shift your heart's focus from the daily to the Divine, from the world to the Word. If you focus on God's truth, you'll find contentment. But if you're obsessed with noticing everything that's wrong with your life, you'll never be able to see all that's right with it.

So pay attention to your heart! Proverbs 4:23 says, "Above all else, guard your heart, for everything you do flows from it."

When you begin to *phroneo* on things above, your heart will seek after the things that honor God and the thoughts that are true. The everyday will become astounding. It will be harder and harder to let corrupt thinking into your life. You'll be writing truth on a dry-ing slab of concrete!

Now, don't expect to be able to change your thinking right away. It's a process—a daily process. It takes time just like it takes time for concrete to set. But once concrete *is* set, it takes an earthquake or a jackhammer to change it, doesn't it? It's the same way with your heart. Once it's set, it can't easily be altered.

Where you set your affection is where you find your satisfaction. Where you set your affection is where you find your identity. Girl, we gotta *phroneo* on things above!

So set your mind on the truth and refuse to settle for lies. Don't get stuck thinking about your mistakes, your imperfections, your insecurities. Instead seek out the amazing in the familiar and the miraculous in the everyday.

The next time you start to feel a twinge of incorrect thinking, imagine that your mind is always in the process of setting like slowly drying concrete. Don't get set on a lie! Immediately shift that cor-rupt thinking back to correct thinking.

When you keep your focus on Jesus, you have peace. Isaiah 26:3 (ESV) tells us, "You keep him in perfect peace whose mind is [set] on you, because he trusts in you." When you set your mind and your affection on things above, you won't have to wonder who you are. And you'll never wander away from the truth of God's love for you. You won't be missing out on anything because you'll be exactly where God wants you to be, doing exactly what He wants you to do. There's nothing more exciting than that!

#truth

Take me by the hand;
Lead me down the path of truth.
You are my Savior, aren't you?
—PSALM 25:5 MSG

Megan told herself, *It's not really a lie. It's just not quite, exactly, specifically, completely the truth.*

Megan had been invited to spend the night at Kathryn's house. She was just getting to know Kathryn and really liked her. Kathryn was outgoing and always wore really cute clothes, and rumor had it she lived in a mansion. She was a year older than Megan, and Megan was flattered that the older girl chose to hang out with her.

There was only one small problem. Megan's parents had a rule that she could only spend the night at a friend's house if adults were going to be home. When Megan asked Kathryn if her parents would be there, she found out that Kathryn's parents were out of town for the weekend.

"But my older sister will be there," Kathryn had said. "She's seventeen so that counts as an adult. Just tell your parents yes."

"Well, " Megan had replied noncommittally, "maybe."

"Seriously, Megan? It's not *that* big a deal! My sister is totally responsible! Come on, just tell your parents yes. It's not like we're going to do anything bad."

Now Megan had a decision to make. Tell her parents that adults would be home (and really, the older sister was *almost* technically an adult) and make Kathryn happy or let her parents know what the real situation was, risk making Kathryn mad, and miss out on a totally fun night.

They wouldn't find out just this once, Megan argued to herself. *And I really want to spend the night at Kathryn's.*

.·~~~··~~~·.

Have you ever been like Megan and told yourself, *just this once*? You know deep down that what you're doing—not telling your parents the truth or copying your classmate's paper or deleting your friend's text that you really don't want to answer—is wrong, but what you want right in that moment seems more important. You *want* to spend the night at your friend's house (and next time you can tell your parents that yes, an adult will be home). You *want* to get a good grade on that paper (and next time you'll do the work yourself because you won't be quite so busy). You *want* to answer your friend's text (but right now you just don't want to deal with any drama).

Gomer was another girl who told herself *just this once*. I imagine that on that one evening when Hosea was out of town preaching and Gomer had asked a neighbor to watch the kids, she believed she was sneaking back to the bad neighborhood where she used to live *just for a visit*. And when she talked to that one guy, she imagined it to be just one little harmless flirtation over dinner. *We're old friends,* she reasoned. *It's no big deal to have dinner together.* Then she hurried home to tuck her children into bed. *That was fun, but it won't happen again*, she promised herself.

But *just this once* led to a second time and a third and...Well, Gomer was becoming a gone girl. She kept making up excuses about needing to run an errand. She loved the buzz of being free and having guys pay attention to her. She was caught up in the moment, having fun, and things seemed to be going her way. At least that's what she kept telling herself.

Somewhere in her mind, Gomer had made the shift. She'd stopped seeing the truth of her situation—beloved wife of Hosea and lucky mom of three adorable kids—and had stopped seeing her true self. She'd started looking into the messed-up mirror of the world, and she was believing its lies. *It may not be right*, Gomer probably reasoned, *but at least I feel like somebody again.*

Remember Megan at the beginning of this chapter? It wasn't right for her to lie to her parents, but she was tempted to because Kathryn made her feel like *somebody*. Kathryn was a popular girl, and Megan wanted to be just like her. She wanted to be accepted, to be known, to be *somebody*.

Just like Megan was losing sight of her true self—a girl who did the right thing, which included being truthful and choosing the right kind of friends—Gomer lost sight of her true self. She made the mistake of thinking that others could give her something more than what Hosea had given her. The Bible says Gomer left Hosea for other lovers because she thought they would give her "my bread and my water, my wool and my flax, my oil and my drink" (Hosea 2:5b NASB).

Bread and water? Wool and flax? Oil and drink? Sounds like a shopping list from ancient times, doesn't it? What does it have to do with what we're talking about?

Yeah, I know. A shopping list is a weird reason for a girl like Gomer to walk away from her marriage, her kids, and her true identity. But the book of Hosea is not only a historical record—it's poetry too. And do you remember what you learned about poetry in school? The images—the word pictures—mean something!

So, what do you think Gomer's shopping list actually represented? What was so amazing about bread and water, wool and flax, and oil and drink?

What Do You Want?

Bread and water are the basics of life—you need them to survive. Gomer needed bread and water to feel secure. Sure, she had a roof over her head and food on the table. Hosea did a good job taking care of his family. But maybe Gomer wanted a little bit more—fancy furniture to replace that food-stained sofa, an in-ground pool instead of a backyard sprinkler, a candlelit dinner at her favorite restaurant instead of the pot of homemade soup simmering on the stove.

Have you ever felt the same way? You know you should be grateful for what you have, but when you start looking at cute rooms on Pinterest or peruse the pages of the latest *PBteen* catalog from Pottery Barn, your own space looks pretty lame. And that's when your mind starts wandering.

Now, what about the wool and flax? In Gomer's time, wool and flax were what women used to make linen. You know, clothes! So wool and flax represented Gomer's wardrobe, her appearance, and the physical impression she made on others.

Remember, Hosea was a good provider. His wife wasn't lacking in skirts, sandals, and dresses. Maybe Gomer wanted a little bit more, though—a few brand-name pieces to set her apart. She wanted to be noticed and then noticed some more!

Finally, what about that oil and drink? I think these were included on the shopping list because of the pleasure they brought. Think about the things that are your go-to for pleasure—your favorite music, a super yummy dessert, a cute new pair of earrings. What little treats make you feel happy?

Now, think again about these things on Gomer's "shopping list." Is there anything wrong with bread and water, wool and flax, or oil and drink? Is there anything wrong with wishing your room looked like one of those cute rooms in a catalog—and buying or making some fun pieces to add a little sparkle? Is there anything wrong with wanting and needing clothes—and not just any old clothes but a cute, in-style wardrobe? Is there anything wrong with desiring pleasure—good music, delicious treats, a fun new candle or lotion, or whatever else brings you pleasure? Is there anything wrong with wanting to be noticed by those around you?

No way! All those things can be *good* things. God wired you to want good things because He wants to give you good things. He created you to need those good things because ultimately they reveal that you need Him—the giver of all good things.

Did Hosea give Gomer good things that brought her pleasure along with all the attention she deserved? Yes! But Gomer wanted what she didn't have, not what she had. Even though she had plenty, it wasn't enough.

When I overlook truth,
I will see only what I lack.

What things do you think you want? Popular friends? A boyfriend? Cute clothes? High-end makeup? Perfect grades? Success in sports? A nice car? Gorgeous hair and skin? A résumé full of impressive activities and amazing accomplishments?

When you think about the things you want the most—the things that influence you—ask yourself, *Do I want these things instead of God or along with God?* Really think about that. You can be honest here. We have nothing to hide! Every girl struggles with this even if she doesn't want to admit it.

We know we should want what God wants for us, but sometimes we hear other voices—our friends, social media, ads on TV—a lot louder than we hear the truth of God's Word. Have you heard some of the same voices I have?

- You aren't smart enough.
- She's prettier than you are.
- If you're not perfect, nobody will like you.
- If you perform well, everyone will love you.
- Nobody even notices you.

When you hear these voices, it's hard to feel like somebody. It seems impossible to find your identity. And what about feeling seen and known and appreciated? Forget about that!

So let's be totally honest with ourselves as we figure this identity thing out. We're all in this together.

Getting Honest

I wonder how honest Gomer was with herself when she was trying to figure out her identity. Because without honesty, there's no freedom. And we all want to be free—free to be the beloved girls of God that He intended us to be.

If we don't embrace the astounding truth that we're seen by God, we'll end up like Gomer, who risked getting noticed in all the wrong ways. You might say "I do" to God—like Gomer said "I do" to Hosea—but you could be living "I'm not." *I'm not loved. I'm not important. I'm not noticed. I'm not seen. I'm not even visible!*

The reality? The opposite of all these things! You *are* loved. You *are* important. You *are* noticed. You *are* seen. You *are* visible.

Once Gomer said "I do" to Hosea, she was no longer Gomer the party girl. She was Gomer the beloved wife. She didn't have to go anywhere else to get her needs met. She didn't have to find herself. All she needed to do was realize that she was already found.

How about you? What do you already have in God that you're looking for in something else or someone else? What's the part of your true identity that you're still seeking?

I'll tell you what I seek. I keep a reminder of it on a shelf in my office, and on my really down days, I keep it in the pocket of my purse so I can carry it with me wherever I go. It's an eight-letter word—eight Scrabble letters glued in place on a Scrabble game ledge. It might look like a cute little craft, but it means so much to me!

A few years ago, my friend Lisa texted me a question, "If one word could become a reality in your life, what would it be?"

I texted her back, "What do you mean?"

"You pick the word you most want as a reality in your life," Lisa answered. "Only you know what it means to you."

This took me the longest time to figure out! The one word that kept popping into my mind was *accepted*, but I was too embarrassed to admit that *accepted* was my word.

Crazy, huh? I was insecure enough to think that Lisa might reject me if she knew I wanted to be accepted! Now, Lisa is about the most loving, accepting friend I have. My hesitation wasn't a reflection on her—it was a reflection on me and how much pressure I felt to be perfect in order to be accepted. My messed-up belief was that I was acceptable only when I was impressive. Obviously, I had not truly identified with my identity!

Accepted is who I already am. Acceptance is what I already have. But acceptance is also what I seek. It's what I long for.

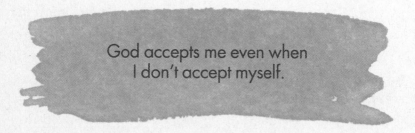

God accepts me even when
I don't accept myself.

Now that I've shared my word with you, think about what your own word might be. What is it that you already have in God that you're still seeking in other people and places? Try to narrow it down to just one word and then write it down.

Think of it this way. What if you constantly seek out cute clothes and accessories to make you happy? What is it that you're really searching for that you already have in God? Could your word be *satisfaction*?

Or maybe you have a superstrong need to have perfect grades and perfect attendance, be a perfect athlete or dancer or musician, and, well, do everything perfectly. What is it that you already have in God that you're trying so hard to find through your achievements? Could it be *admiration*?

Perhaps you feel invisible to your parents, friends, teachers, or coaches and try hard—too hard—to make them notice you. What is it that you're after that you already have in God? Could it be *attention*?

Have you decided on *your* word yet? If you own a Scrabble game, go ahead and pull out the letter tiles that spell your word and sit them on the ledge so you can be reminded. My Scrabble word *accepted* always reminds me that I already have what I want. When I'm feeling less than accepted, I hold it in my hand, wrap my fingers around it, and tell myself, *This is what God gave me! This is who I am!*

Can we take just a moment right here to think about how awesome God is and how much He loves us? He's already given us acceptance and everything else we need!

Just like Lisa glued the word *accepted* to a Scrabble ledge for me, you can ask God to glue your own word to your heart so that with every heartbeat, you feel the truth of His love for you. And you'll come to accept the truth of who you are and all that you have in Him. With every heartbeat, you'll feel the truth of His love for you.

Every day remember your word! If we don't identify with our true identity on a daily basis, we forget who we are. We forget who God made us to be, and we wander away from Him to look for acceptance and significance apart from Him.

We all need our bread and water, wool and flax, and oil and drink. It's just that we already have absolutely all that we need in God. But what we feel we haven't received from Him, we try to get on our own. Hosea wrote that we "rejected what is good" (Hosea 8:3).

When we're going after our own needs and ignoring everything that God has provided for us, we're not acting out of our identity. We're acting out of our *iddiction*.

Iddiction

Iddiction? Is that a typo? A word from another language? What in the world is *iddiction*? Never heard of it? That's okay! It's a Jennifer-ism!

When we girls set our hearts on things below—the things that the world says will make us happy—we feel dissatisfied. We're painfully aware of our own insecurity. We might as well be invisible!

Now, we know we shouldn't feel this way. But our feelings are hard to ignore because, truth be told, we're on our own minds a lot! And we're naturally drawn to anything or anyone that gives us the sense of self we lack. (Remember how being around Kathryn made Megan feel more important?) We're all a little like Gomer. We're all *iddicts*.

So what's an iddict? An iddict is someone who finds her identity in herself rather than in God. An iddict wants her own way. She goes after her own wants. She trusts in her own wisdom. She does things the way *she* wants to do them!

We become iddicts when we reject our true identity and God's wisdom and ways. We become iddicts when we buy more stuff or get involved in more activities so we can satisfy ourselves. We become iddicts when we find our sense of worth in the latest fashion, a perfect report card, or our impressive social media standing. We become iddicts when we do whatever we can—whatever it takes— to be accepted.

An iddict looks for her identity in herself, not in God. She sees the girl she's trying to make herself be, not the girl who God wants her to be.

Remember how I tried to find acceptance, identity, and value in what others thought of me on social media? Hello. My name is Jennifer, and I am an iddict! I am addicted to *me*—my ways, my wants, my wisdom!

Yes, I definitely have those days when I think that my way, my wants, and my wisdom are good enough. If life is good, I am good, and I don't need God for anything. But oh, girl! If I feel less than enough or insecure, if I'm having a bad hair day or I make a mistake or I lose a friend, well, then my iddiction shows up because I've totally lost my sense of self.

This is a good time to remember your reality. You are a chosen, loved girl of God. That's the identity you need to identify with!

But, you know, we just happen to be human. And sometimes our iddiction is stronger than our identity. So while we're forever begging God and others to accept us, we mess up. We start seeking acceptance in all the wrong places, and then all we feel is "except me"! *God loves everyone...except me. Everyone is so perfect...except me. Everyone is worthy...except me. Everyone is somebody...except me.*

Don't believe those lies for a minute!

Rejecting the Lies

Yep, we iddicts tend to forget what is right or true. And that includes forgetting what is right or true about ourselves! When we overlook who we truly are and who God truly is, we feel invisible. No doubt about it!

An important thing to remember about iddiction is that it's not based on truth. Iddiction is totally 100 percent based on lies. Let me share with you three lies that iddicts believe—lies I have believed— so you can recognize (and reject) them next time you see them.

Lie #1: Who I am and what I struggle with are the same thing.

It might make sense to think, *If I fail, I'm a failure.* But that's not true! We all make mistakes, but our mistakes don't have to define us. They can *refine* us. They can help us learn and grow and mature. We are who God says we are, and we are not all our failures! You may feel rejected or left out or like a loser (or fill in your own word), but that doesn't mean you *are* any of those things.

Instead think of who you *truly* are—an amazing girl of God—and then tell yourself the truth: *I am God's beloved daughter. I am chosen. I matter to Him!*

Lie #2: Who I am and what I do are the same thing.

We're human *beings*, not human *doings*, aren't we? Our identity isn't based on what we do. It's based on what God did for us. If we base our sense of self on our popularity, our grades, or our accomplishments, we risk losing our sense of self if and when those things change. So instead, we need to base our identity on what will never, ever change—the truth of God's Word and His everlasting love for us. We simply need to receive who we are from God and not achieve a status from everyone else.

Lie #3: Who I am is not good enough.

When we're driven by our own performance rather than by God's provisions, we live with a "not good enough" mentality. We tell ourselves that we must perform—in school, in our activities, in our social life—to be accepted. That's a lot of pressure to put on ourselves! And we can get super stressed out when we believe this lie.

Do you want to hear something very cool? God tells us that He has already performed on our behalf—and His provision is sufficient. When we feel the need to be more, we can rest in the truth that God is enough—more than enough!

Be careful not to trust your own opinion of yourself—or someone else's opinion of you—more than you trust God and His opinion of you. He will tell you the truth of who you are!

Girl, let's help each other believe the truth! When we know and believe God's truth, we're set free from iddiction. We know our true identity. And we realize we had what we were searching for all along.

The "just this once" excuse—like the "not quite" truth that Megan wanted to tell her parents—isn't so tempting when you can see the truth with clear eyes! So look into the mirror of God's Word and see the beautiful reflection of your real self. *That's* the true you!

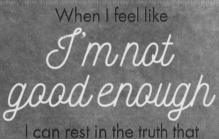

When I feel like

I'm not good enough

I can rest in the truth that

God is more than enough.

#TheInvisibleBook

#real

Trust GOD from the bottom of your heart; don't try to figure out everything on your own. Listen for GOD's voice in everything you do, everywhere you go; he's the one who will keep you on track. Don't assume that you know it all.

—PROVERBS 3:5-7 MSG

So far Faith had had an easy time filling out her camp counselor application. She'd listed her grades (pretty good), school activities (nothing too impressive, but she'd jotted down a few clubs and sports), and work experience (mainly babysitting and pet-sitting jobs for neighbors). She'd gotten letters of recommendation from her youth pastor and her favorite science teacher. Now she just needed to write the essay.

Faith stared at the paper while chewing on her pencil. *In 500 words or less, please write an essay using the following prompt: Who am I?* Faith was stuck. *Who am I?* Well, she was Faith! But beyond that she didn't really know. She was a student, but so was everybody else applying to be a camp counselor! She'd been somewhat involved with school activities, but she was certain others had done way more. And did babysitting and pet-sitting really count as work experience?

Gazing at the blank page, Faith's mind drifted. *I can't think of anything that would make me stand out. I'm not a straight-A student. I'm not captain of the soccer team or student body president. I've never had a real job.*

Was she supposed to write about her love for the color blue or her passion for hiking in the rain or her obsession with making sure all her friends received handmade cards on their birthdays? Probably not, but that was who she was!

What does the camp want me to be? Who am I, anyway? Should I make something up? After all, there isn't anything terribly impressive about the real me!

·⁓~ꭑℓꭓ~⁓·

Have you ever been faced with a situation where you're expected to define yourself—in 500 words or less? Even if you've never had to put the words down on paper, you've probably wondered the same thing Faith has: *Who is the real me?*

You know the brand name Coca-Cola, right? Of course you do! Well, for 99 years, the Coca-Cola Company had been selling its famous drink popularly known as Coke. Coca-Cola was the leader of all soft drink companies with skyrocketing sales, and their existing Coke formula was selling briskly. But do you know what Coca-Cola did in 1985? After almost a hundred years of making Coke the exact same way, the company changed the recipe! They announced they were going to introduce a newer, sweeter drink that would replace the real thing.

This was some serious stuff! (If you're from the South like me, you will totally agree. You don't mess with my Coke!)

Well, the company released the "new Coke," and guess what happened? After 40,000 letters of complaint, a ton of unhappy phone calls, and a boatload of bad reviews, it took Coca-Cola only three months to announce the return of Coke "Classic." You just can't replace the real thing!

That's what we do, though, when we try to replace what God wants for us with what we want for ourselves. God's plan is the real thing. Our plan? It's a pretty lame attempt to figure out what exactly *is* real.

When we feel invisible—when we start asking ourselves, *Who am I?*—is when we start trying to replace the Real Thing with our own thing.

Back in Gomer's day, people often replaced the Real Thing—God—with idols of their own making. Of course, life is different for us now. We don't start building giant golden calves in our yards or setting up shrines to Baal in our bedrooms.

But we still make and worship idols. Really and truly! When we take our material possessions, our accomplishments, or people we admire and put too much emphasis on them, we actually make idols—little gods—out of them. And when we give these things an unhealthy amount of attention or influence over our lives, that's the same thing as worshipping them.

When we take what we want in life and put that above what God wants for us, we create what I call *Gomerisms*. (Isn't it fun to make up new words?) Gomerisms always, always put us on the wrong path because they pull us away from the Real Thing and instead draw our attention to shallow substitutes.

I like to put Gomerisms into three groups. First, *trusting in my own wisdom* is a Gomerism. Second, *elevating my own wants* is a Gomerism. And third, *demanding my own way* is a Gomerism.

Gomerisms might sound like bad things (especially with a name like that!), but they aren't always bad.

The Right Thing

The main idea of a Gomerism isn't necessarily a bad thing. Desiring our own wisdom, wants, and way is human nature! But because we're prone to wander away from God, we can get super confused about what the *right* thing is. Got questions? Stick with me. I'll explain!

Your Wisdom

When you hear the word *wisdom*, what comes to mind? A perfect report card? An old book of stories that teaches life lessons (preferably read to you by a wise old grandparent)? What the winner of a science or math competition needs to have?

You possess wisdom—wisdom given to you by God! He gave you a good mind, and He wants you to use it. So, while it's right to use your brain and think for yourself, it's wrong to trust *only* in your own wisdom. Proverbs 3:5-6 (NASB) says, "Trust in the LORD with all your heart and do not lean on your own understanding. In all your ways acknowledge Him, and He will make your paths straight."

God's Word clearly tells us to trust Him above anything else—the wisdom of adults, the wisdom of leaders, the wisdom of ourselves. When we consider any other kind of wisdom equal to—or above—God's wisdom, we'll end up choosing our way over His way. And that way leads to nothing but trouble!

Your Wants

At just about any online store, you can either add items to a shopping cart or a wish list. Sometimes it's fun to add thousands of dollars' worth of merchandise to our favorite store's wish list even if we don't plan on spending one penny! But be careful about those wishes. It's fine to acknowledge that you want things—like when you tell your grandma what you would love to have for your birthday or you pray that you'll do well on your math test—but we should never elevate our own wants above everything and everyone else.

Here's what God's Word says about this: "Do nothing out of selfish ambition or vain conceit. Rather, in humility value others above yourselves, not looking to your own interests but each of you to the interests of the others" (Philippians 2:3-4).

If you put what *you* want above what other people need and what God wants for you, that's only going to make you more into yourself. And the more you're on your own mind, the more self-aware and self-absorbed—and way less happy—you're going to be. That's the way it always works!

Your Way

While it might be reasonable to *desire* your own way, it's wrong to *demand* it. Why? Because God says His way—not your way—is perfect: "As for God, his way is perfect: The Lord's word is flawless; he shields all who take refuge in him" (Psalm 18:30).

It's hard to not want your own way when you're surrounded by people who are used to thinking of themselves first. Everyone is trying to fit in, to find their place, to understand who they are. It's only natural that we try to figure out what our way is—and then go for it.

> God's way is perfect.
> Mine...not so much!

But only God's way is guaranteed perfect. My own way? Not so much. We might *think* we're following our heart and doing what's best for ourselves, but we can never trust completely in our own hearts. That's because it's so easy for our emotions to fool us. So look to God's heart first and see if your way matches up with His way.

Your *wisdom*. Your *wants*. Your *way*. Remember what I named these things? Gomerisms! Which one do you struggle with the most? Which one has caused you the most trouble—in your friendships, in your relationship with your family, in your own heart and the way you feel about yourself?

Going for It!

We all have our own Gomerisms that the GPS of our soul navigates toward. Some of us take pride in our own wisdom. We're smart, and we have the grades and test scores to prove it, so why not use the amazing brain God gave us? Many of us are gifted with determination and drive, so for us it's all about our own wants. No matter the situation, there's no doubt what we want—and we want it *now*!

For me, demanding my own way is the Gomerism that tends to rear its ugly head and cause problems, especially in my relationships with others. Have you been there too, arguing with your siblings, your parents, or even your best friend?

Maybe you and your sister are both *always* right—neither of you is ever wrong! What's more, you both always have the only right opinion. The problem is you don't *share* that same opinion. But you both stubbornly cling to the belief that your way is the best way, and—funny how this works—your way and your sister's way are never the same way!

Over the years I've learned that my way is not all it's cracked up to be. It's not always the best way. And it's definitely not the *only* way. But when I feel insecure or invisible, I tend to act out of my iddiction and start demanding my own way. That's how I try to feel seen, acknowledged, and accepted. But it never works.

It gets even worse when I try to keep track of the times I didn't get my own way. When I do this, I'm not acting out of my identity as the beloved and chosen of God—someone who has the ability to forgive and then give in (if that's the right thing to do). I am, instead, acting as an iddict.

But then there are those amazing times when we hear what God is asking us to do, and we *do* act out of our true identity. We realize that compared to our friendship with our sister or our relationship with our parents, getting our own way just isn't all that important.

When you act out of your God-given identity, you're all about God's way of love and other-centeredness. You can imagine how much better things are between you and other people when this happens!

So start to really and truly notice which of your Gomerisms—your wisdom, your wants, or your way—are showing up. Figure out when they tend to appear and discover where they're doing the most damage.

A good way to begin to identify your Gomerisms is by noticing the thought patterns that usually follow a Gomerism: *Ugh, I shouldn't have! Man, I wish I wouldn't have! Oh, if I just could have!*

Basically you feel regret—regret about the things you did, the things you said, or the choices you made. You know it's a Gomerism when you wish you could restart, redo, or delete!

So how can you avoid the "woulda, coulda, shoulda" of Gomerisms? I've found it's really helpful to ask myself three different questions before I do anything I'm unsure of: *Could I be wrong? Would I recommend? Should I rethink?*

Could I Be Wrong?

Once you've identified the Gomerism—or Gomerisms—that are giving you the most trouble, stop yourself as soon as you see you're going there again. Then ask yourself one of these questions: *Could demanding my own way right now be wrong? Could elevating my own wants in this situation be wrong? Could trusting my own heart—and my own wisdom—be wrong?*

What you're doing here is asking yourself one simple question: *Could I be wrong?*

If your answer is anything but a major *no*, give yourself more time before taking any action. It's never wrong to stop and think about your motivation or your actions. And it might just save you a lot of grief or heartache!

Would I Recommend?

When you feel tempted to be Gomeristic, ask yourself if you would recommend the way you're tempted to think or act to your best friend or your brother or even your parent. Ask yourself how you would feel if you saw them acting like that!

Would you tell your best friend to behave the way you're tempted to behave at that moment? Would that behavior make her feel positive about herself and others? Would you recommend that your mom or dad act the way you're about to act? What would you think of them if they acted that way? What's more, how would you like to be on the receiving end of that action? If it seems silly to picture these things, it probably means you wouldn't recommend them!

If you wouldn't recommend your thoughts or your behavior to someone else, chances are you don't need to think or behave that way either! So take a moment to reflect and pray before you do something you might regret. Ask God to remind you who you are so you can act out of your true identity, not your iddiction.

Should I Rethink?

I'll be the first to admit that it's impossible to think before every single word you speak (or text or tweet or...), to *really* think through what you're saying in each individual word. But once you've figured out which Gomerism you struggle with the most, you can put your brain and your heart on high alert to be aware of thinking before you say or do or write something you'll totally regret.

If you realize that in specific places or with certain people, you tend to act out of your iddiction (like when you're with people who always seem to push every insecurity button you have), get ready to rethink your thinking! Tell yourself, *I'm going to rethink so I don't regret!*

Rethink why you might insist on demanding your own way, if that's what you usually do in this situation. Rethink why you put your wants above what others might want or need—or what God wants for you. Rethink why you ultimately listen to your own heart and trust in your own wisdom before listening to God or others who have your best interest in mind.

And then ask yourself again, *Should I rethink?* The answer to that question, most of the time, is *yes*! You don't want to regret sending that text or making that choice or getting into that argument. So *rethink*!

God's Way and My Way

As you get good at recognizing your favorite Gomerisms, you can ask God to help you start making the shift from acting out of your iddiction to acting out of your identity. A great way to see if you're heading for a Gomerism is to replace the word *my* with *Thy*.

Yeah, I know! *Thy* is a King James, totally old-fashioned kind of word, but it rhymes nicely with *my*. And the rhyme is easy to remember, so let's just go with it.

I'm using *Thy* to represent God. When you start to wander off your own way, stop and remind yourself that you're all about God's way. And say this out loud: *Jesus, I choose Thy way over my way. I choose Thy wisdom over my wisdom. I choose Thy wants and desires over my wants and desires.*

The really cool thing here is that the more you act out of your identity—an amazing, beloved girl of God—the sooner "my" and "Thy" will become the same thing! In other words, God's way will become your way. God's wants will become your wants. God's wisdom will become your wisdom. I just love that!

Your iddiction will start to lose its power because you aren't feeding it with as many lies. You'll become more confident in your true identity. You'll grow into the girl God created you to be!

The problem with Gomerisms is that they encourage us to wander. And that kind of wandering never takes us where we want to go. It never leads us to who we really want to be—who we already are in Christ.

Gomerisms also yank us farther away from our Source of self—God Himself. And remember what happens when we leave our Source of self? We lose our sense of self! We have no idea who we are, how we're supposed to act, and what we're supposed to do. We find ourselves asking, *Who am I, anyway?*

So go, go, go away, Gomerisms! You ain't welcome here no more!

The very last verse in the book of Hosea says, "If you want to live well, make sure you understand all this. If you know what's good for you, you'll learn this inside and out. GOD's paths get you where you want to go. Right-living people walk them easily; wrong-living people are always tripping and stumbling" (Hosea 14:9 MSG).

Girl, God's paths *do* get us where we want to go. And they lead us to actually *be* who we *are*—beloved, incredible, amazing girls of God!

Now, let me tell you one more thing before we wrap up this chapter. When I first stumbled on this thing I call iddiction, I was bummed. I thought, *I should know better! I should be past this! I should be getting it by now!*

I was super frustrated and totally ashamed that what I thought was low self-esteem was actually high self-awareness—self-absorption, actually. Remember me, myself, and I? And when I realized that the times I felt the most invisible were usually the times I was the most self-absorbed, I was embarrassed.

> When I feel the most invisible,
> I'm only looking at myself.

No girl wants to think she's selfish. We all want to think we've grown less selfish as we've grown closer to God. And we have! But as long as we live on this earth, there will always be some kind of iddiction in us. The problem is that at first it's hard to know what to do with it or how to change it. Sometimes we have no clue what to do!

Sure, you can start to identify the lies and focus on the truth, but that doesn't always take care of the problem completely. And it doesn't take care of it right away. There is, however, something you can do that really and truly works.

If you're starting to see that the times you feel the most invisible are the times you're totally focused on yourself, please be patient with yourself! If you're realizing that your low self-esteem could actually be high self-awareness, know that everything is going to be okay!

Because iddicts live with that big letter *I*, we can be quick to condemn ourselves: *"I" am such a loser! "I" am not good enough! "I" will never amount to anything! "I" am always making mistakes! "I" don't even know who "I" am!*

But try not to let the *I* in iddiction speak too loudly, sweet girl! After all, *I* is smack-dab in the middle of the word *lie.*

Let your *I* be found where it should be—hidden in Chr-i-st! In Christ is where your true identity is found. That is the one place you are never, ever invisible!

When I act out of
my identity,
God's way will become
my way.
God's way will become
my wants.
God's way will become
my wisdom.

#TheInvisibleBook

#faithful

*Love GOD, your God, with your whole
heart: love him with all that's in you,
love him with all you've got!*
—DEUTERONOMY 6:5 MSG

As Emily saw Cassie enter the choir room, she thought, *Please don't
sit by me again. You sat by me last week, and I really need to start making some new friends.*

Sure enough, though, Cassie made a beeline for Emily the second
she saw her. Impossible to miss in her neon yellow shirt and bright
pink floral leggings, Cassie was a little bit...different. Emily had been
grateful to have someone show her the ropes on her first day of choir
practice, and Cassie was certainly an enthusiastic guide. She knew
everything about everything—and she let everyone know it!

But three weeks later, Emily still felt like the new girl. She noticed
that most of the other girls in the choir gave Cassie a wide berth.
Nobody was mean to her—not exactly. There might have been a little bit of whispering and giggling going on, but Emily never heard
anyone make rude comments out loud.

Cassie was just one of those people who eventually got on everyone's nerves. She talked too loud. She dressed, well, creatively. She let everyone know her opinion about everything. She even tried to correct the choir director! Sure, Cassie had been friendly and helpful when Emily was new to choir, but hanging out with her was getting to be draining. And Emily didn't like how people looked at her—or how she imagined they looked at her—when she was with Cassie.

Do they think I'm like Cassie? Emily wondered. *Will anyone else want to be my friend now? Should I stop hanging out with her? Should I tell her she can't sit by me? I don't want to be mean, but I have no clue what to do!*

.·ᴖ⁓ᴖ.

Even if you've never been the new girl, you might have experienced an identity crisis like Emily did. Maybe you have a friend or a sibling who's different, someone who draws attention to herself, and you feel there's nothing in the world worse than standing out. You just want to blend in!

Emily wanted to avoid Cassie's attention and blend in. Even though she thought she was focusing on Cassie and the other girls in the choir, she was actually focusing on herself. When we spend our time obsessing about what others might think of us, we're focusing on what we want and who we are. And as long as we keep the focus on ourselves, we'll never be satisfied.

The Faulty Bow

You'll never be content if your focus is only on *you*. When you're determined to follow your own way, elevate your own wants, and trust solely in your own wisdom (remember those from the last chapter?), you'll never be truly happy. That's what happened to Gomer. That's what was starting to happen to Emily. That's what can happen to us.

Have you ever shot an arrow with a bow? If you have, you know that it takes practice to make your arrow go straight. And it takes even more practice to hit your intended target. Without practice it's easy to see your arrows landing in some crazy places! But even if you're really good at archery, sometimes your arrows still don't hit their target. And sometimes that's not the archer's fault. Sometimes the bow itself is messed up, and even if the archer is super skilled, the arrows still land in the wrong place. A bow like this is called a *faulty* bow.

Did you know that when we're set on focusing only on ourselves and wanting our own way, we can become like a faulty bow? I bet you've never been called a faulty bow before, have you? Well, let me do a little explaining here!

The Bible compares God's people—which includes us—to a faulty bow. "They do not turn to the Most High; they are like a faulty bow" (Hosea 7:16). This is a pretty and poetic way of saying that we're misguided and, therefore, unreliable.

When we're functioning as a faulty bow, we're bent our own way. We're thinking only of ourselves without considering God or those around us. And when using our faulty bows, we shoot our arrows and hope they hit our intended target. But they never do. A faulty bow's arrows never land in the right place.

When we're operating as a faulty bow, we search for our identity apart from Christ—an identity that we think everyone will like—but we end up having no clue who we really are.

> When I try to be
> who everyone thinks I should be,
> I will have no clue
> who I really am.

We shoot random arrows, hoping to hit what makes us happy, but we keep needing more and more to make us feel satisfied. We aim for the target of acceptance, but what we hit is a whole bunch of insecurity. We're desperate to be seen, acknowledged, and appreciated, but we end up feeling jealous, envious, and invisible.

Do you see what I mean here? We might be aiming for the right thing, but our arrows are landing in the wrong place. And then we have no clue what to do! This is what's going to happen to poor Gomer—aiming for satisfaction, she eventually lands in slavery.

Have you ever made a choice or acted in a way that seemed fine at first, but then your choice or your action ended up making you feel ashamed or disappointed?

Let's say you love to shop. You feel happy and excited when you buy the things you want—a cute top, some sparkly nail polish, flip-flops in your favorite color. But then you're totally out of money and you question if you really needed all that stuff and think maybe you should have saved your money and spent it on something you really needed.

What about eating junk food? A candy bar and a blended coffee drink—you know, one of those drinks that's basically a bunch of sugar with a little caffeine in it—might seem like a great lunchtime pick-me-up. After all, it's hard to stay awake in your afternoon history class. But after the initial sugar buzz wears off, you're exhausted—and you still have another class to get through *plus* cross-country practice. Maybe that quick, pick-me-up lunch wasn't such a good idea after all!

The things that at first make us feel free can end up making us feel stuck. We didn't get what we were aiming for. We got something else entirely!

Hosea said that's what happens when we function as faulty bows. "They sow the wind and reap the whirlwind" (Hosea 8:7). This means that we're after one thing—something we're sure we want—but we end up getting something we never intended to get.

Now, please remember that the things you want aren't *always* wrong. They just have the potential to go wrong when you're a faulty bow.

Think about it this way. God is the Master Archer. You are the bow in His hands. Just as an archer places arrows in a bow, God places desires, longings, drives, callings, and gifts in you. A desire for pleasure—like a yummy coffee drink or a cute new pair of shoes—is a normal, healthy desire. Longing to be accepted by your peers is a natural part of being a teen. A drive to do your best—to get straight A's or be the first-chair flute in band—is a God-given drive. There's nothing wrong with these things!

The problem comes when we're functioning as a faulty bow and operating outside of God's expertise. That's when our desires go off track and our arrows hit everything but the target we're intending them to hit. That's because we're thinking only of ourselves and focusing only on our own wants. So we might spend our money on things we really don't need and later regret spending it. We might act a little bit fake to be accepted by a certain group of peers and then later regret becoming a part of that group. We might skip youth group or a really great service project so we can study or practice just a little bit more to become number one and then regret the amazing experience we missed out on.

Have you ever looked at your life and thought, *How did I get here? When did I become this self-absorbed? How come I'm so insecure? Why do I always feel invisible? Why can't I ever feel good enough?* We've all had those thoughts!

When you start asking yourself those questions, check your bow! Is it in God's hands, or are you holding it yourself and bending it out of shape as you so desperately try to get what you think you want?

The worst thing about the faulty bow is where its arrows land. Often they land in a minefield!

The Minefield of Competitiveness

All of us have a drive to do well, to be noticed, and to be acknowledged for our efforts. But when we act out of our iddiction instead of our identity (remember that?), our arrows are going to end up in the minefield of *competitiveness*.

Now, competitiveness isn't always a bad thing. Sometimes it's a really good thing, like when you're sprinting to a soccer ball or buckling down and studying for that biology test. But there's a negative side to competitiveness. That side comes out when we constantly compare ourselves to others and find ourselves coming up short every time. Here's how this kind of thinking goes: *If she is good, I have to be better. If she is pretty, I have to be prettier. If she has one pair of brand-name boots, I really should have two pairs. If she has 50 likes on her Instagram post, I need 51, actually 52 just in case I lose one so I'll still be ahead!*

Spelled out like this, it sounds totally ridiculous, but you get the idea. When we don't feel complete in Christ, we compete with others. God never intended for us to live like this, though, even as self-aware, highly driven teen girls! Remember, you're not a faulty bow. You're a faithful bow! So if you've been finding yourself tiptoe-ing through a minefield of competitiveness, try this. *Compliment instead of compete.*

> When I don't feel complete in Christ, I compete with others.

Begin complimenting the girls you're secretly (or not so secretly) competing against. Compliment someone for that quality you're actually jealous of. Instead of thinking, *I can't stand you because you're so smart*, say, "Great job on that paper! Maybe we can study together sometime." And then pass on the compliment to some-one else. "Hannah is such a good writer! Did you hear her read her paper? She must have worked really hard on it!" Even if you never speak a word to the girl you've found yourself competing against, you can think complimentary thoughts about her every time that jealous feeling starts to creep into your mind.

You want to feel good about yourself and good about others, right? Well if you're finding yourself in constant competition, you'll never get what you're aiming for. But when you make the choice to compliment instead of compete, you'll actually begin to really and truly like yourself. Being kind to others instead of feeling envious of them will actually become totally natural.

When you decide to make the change from competing to com-plimenting, your faulty bow becomes a faithful bow. Then you'll find yourself right where you want to be—happy about who you are and genuinely happy for others.

The Minefield of Envy

The next minefield to watch out for is in the territory of *envy*. Although we don't like to admit it, envy is a pretty common thing for us girls to experience, isn't it? I sure don't want to admit to all the times I've felt envious of someone. That's because I don't like what envy says about me! It's a really hard thing to love a friend so much, yet at the same time fight against feeling envious of her. Let's say you have that friend who is so perfectly pretty, so amazingly smart, so effortlessly popular, and so incredibly nice. How could you feel envious of someone who is such a great person? Well, easily, especially if you wish you were more like her!

Now, you can still be her friend and occasionally feel those pangs of envy. But please be careful. Our envy can really get out of control if we let it morph into just plain dislike or resentment. Then if we start to spread rumors of gossip about the girl we're feeling envious of, well, that's definitely a path we need to avoid traveling! It will definitely hurt your friendship with that girl, your relationships with others, and even your relationship with God.

It's also possible that you think you don't like someone at all when deep down all you are is jealous of her. This is very common with girls we haven't bothered getting to know. Sometimes when we're extra critical or resentful of someone, it's because we're envious of her.

Here's the main thing about envy: Envy isn't really about the other person, no matter how perfectly perfect she may seem to be. Envy is actually about us. And the main thing that envy reveals is that we really don't like ourselves very much.

Okay, let's get real here! If you're feeling envious of a friend or even someone you don't really know, that's a symptom of insecurity and discontentment with yourself. Why would you even want to go there if you could avoid it in the first place? No thank you!

If you find yourself constantly fighting feelings of jealousy—wishing you could dress like this girl or be popular like that girl—it's a clue you may be operating as a faulty bow.

Remember, being envious will always make you more self-aware and insecure—not less. An envious person might say something like this: "I can't believe everyone voted for her for class president! She always thinks she's so much better than anyone else!" What's really being said here is this: "I wish *I* had been chosen as class president. I was really hoping for that position. Just look how hard I worked on my campaign! Now I feel like a total loser. I feel invisible because *she's* getting all the attention. I feel embarrassed because probably *nobody* voted for me. And I'm feeling sick inside because I have so many feelings of jealousy—not joy—toward her. Not only do I want to be class president, I also want all the attention and praise she's receiving for winning the election!"

When you look at it like that, it looks pretty unattractive, right? No girl intends to live in envy of others, but when it happens (and believe me, it does), our thoughts can become downright ugly. When we get sucked into thinking this way, we're the only ones who lose. We lose joy and confidence and contentment as we grow in bitterness and anger and self-awareness.

So what you need to do is pick up that arrow, reset your bow, and get far, far away from the minefield of envy! There's only one way to stop your jealous thought patterns and feelings of negativity. The way to do this is by *encouraging*!

When you say, "Awesome! You did an amazing job!" you're being an encouragement. I'll give you a little hint here. Pray before you encourage, and God will put genuine feelings of good into your heart. Really, this works!

By offering pure, no-strings-attached encouragement, you'll feel so much better. God will help develop in you a pure heart and a kind spirit—things that are actually worth envying! And being encouraging to others is a beautiful way to serve Jesus. The more you serve Him, the less you will serve yourself. Your character will grow, and your feelings of insecurity will shrink.

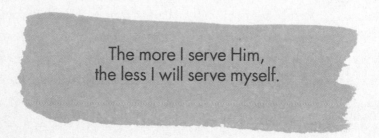

The more I serve Him,
the less I will serve myself.

The Minefield of Feeling Threatened

In the craziness of life, it's pretty easy to have days when we're feeling overly sensitive. Whether it's from stress or hormones or just life in general, it's pretty common for teens to be emotional! But if you find that you're being overly sensitive all the time and it feels like everyone is out to get you, there's a good chance that you're once again operating as a faulty bow. You want to feel special and significant, but you've consistently been landing your arrows in the not-good-enough zone.

God assures us that we never have to feel less than. In His Word He consistently reminds us that through Him we are more than enough. But when we start thinking about the way others treated us—a teacher who wasn't fair, a friend who told someone else your secret, a sister who lost your favorite sweater—it's hard not to feel threatened. Maybe your teacher didn't show you the respect you thought you deserved. Perhaps you felt as if your friend was out to get you or you think your sister never treats you as nicely as you treat her.

If you interpret every suggestion as a slap in the face, every correction as a criticism, and every idea shared with you as an insult to your intelligence, well you're probably landing the arrows from your faulty bow in an exploding minefield!

What can you do when you start to feel threatened and like everyone is out to get you? Choose to be thankful instead! *That sounds nice and easy*, you might think, *but how does it work in real life?*

Start with this one step: Instead of taking everything personally—the comment your teacher made, the secret your friend shared, the sweater your sister borrowed (okay, stole!)—immediately take it to Jesus with a thankful heart. Say, "Thank You, Lord, for teaching me and helping me grow."

Yes, it sounds crazy, but trust me. It works!

If you're feeling threatened by someone, especially someone you're jealous of, thank God for that person's positive attributes. She is who God made her to be, so to resent what is good in her is to resent what God has done in and for her.

I know this is difficult to do! But it's so very important. When you're not being who you are in God's hands—when you're focusing on what you're *not* instead of what you *are*—you will never, ever be satisfied with yourself, your life, your friendships, your goals, your hopes and dreams, or anything else.

When you're threatened by others because you're not thankful for them, you'll never be thankful for *you*. God wants you to be thankful for you. After all He made you! And He is thankful for you! Go ahead and thank God for what He has done in and for someone else and watch your focus shift from who you wish you were to who God is.

When we look to Him, we find ourselves. If you find yourself struggling with competitiveness, envy, or feeling threatened, ask

God to help you right where you're at. Tell Him how you're feeling and then hand your faulty bow over to Him because being your own archer never, ever works. When we forget who we are in the hands of the Master Archer, we start shooting ourselves into the center of everything so we can be seen and feel important.

When we put ourselves first and don't think of others, pride takes over and brings us to a crash landing. As Proverbs 16:18 wisely says, "Pride goes before destruction, a haughty spirit before a fall."

Remember that God doesn't make mistakes! He doesn't create faulty bows. If we choose to accept our identity as a loved, accepted, and complete girl of God, we'll be able to rest in the hands of the Master Archer. His will and His ways will guide us to our target, and we won't twist and turn to get our own way.

When we become faithful bows, we become comfortable with ourselves, imperfections and all. We're comfortable in the skin we're in when we rest in the Hands of God!

So if—well, *when*—you find yourself taking matters into your own hands and doing your own thing, tell yourself, *I need to ask God, my Master Archer, to take control! I can rest in His hands, and He will guide me where I need to go.*

- You won't be tempted to compete anymore. You'll give compliments instead.

- You won't envy anymore. You'll give encouragement instead.

- You won't feel threatened anymore. You'll give thanks instead.

- You won't think only of yourself and what others think of you. You'll have your eyes focused on God and what you can do for others.

When you do this, you'll like what you see when you look in the mirror!

When we put our own wisdom, wants, and will first, we have nothing. But when we rest content in the capable hands of the Master Archer—when we ask Him to bend us His way—we have everything.

We won't worry so much about what others think. We'll be able to form strong and real friendships, and our lives will reflect the faithfulness that's in our hearts.

#ultimategood

*Be cheerful no matter what; pray all
the time; thank God no matter what
happens. This is the way God wants you
who belong to Christ Jesus to live.*
—1 Thessalonians 5:16-18 msg

"Meet me at Starbucks!" read Sarah's text from her best friend, Rebekah. "We need to talk!"

After school Sarah walked the two blocks to Starbucks, ordered a white chocolate mocha, and pulled out her homework to get a few things done before Rebekah—who was always, always late—arrived.

For once, though, Rebekah wasn't late. She came bursting through the door, backpack unzipped and papers spilling out, and plopped down in a seat by the astonished Sarah.

"You sure got here in a hurry!" Sarah said. "What's going on?"

"It's Taylor," Rebekah answered. "I'm worried about her."

Sarah nodded. Their close friend—well, *former* close friend—Taylor had been acting a bit strange lately. Taylor had always been a good student, but lately she'd been skipping class. Midway through track season, she stopped showing up at practice. And she hadn't been coming to youth group very much either. Come to think of it, Sarah couldn't remember the last time she'd seen Taylor in church.

"She's not answering my texts at all," Sarah noted. "I sent a few asking her how she is and what's up, but I haven't heard anything."

"I totally don't want to gossip, but she's been hanging out with Madeline and Angela lately, and I just don't think they're the best influence on her. Know what I mean?"

"True," agreed Sarah, taking a sip of her mocha. "And I saw her riding home from school with that guy Eli. I'm not sure what's going on between them."

"She acts like she's happy, but it seems kinda fake to me. Like she wants everyone to look at her and see how cool she is now. But I know Taylor. I don't think she really wants to be like this."

"I hate confrontation," said Sarah, "but I kind of think we have to do something. And if both of us talk to her together, it might be better."

"Okay," said Rebekah, "but I don't want to hurt her, and I hate drama, so let's pray first. We're going to need some help on this one!"

⚬───⟊───⚬

Sarah and Rebekah's friend Taylor was following her Gomerisms by ignoring her true identity and trying to create a new one—an identity that would bring her more attention and put her in the spotlight. But was she really going where she wanted to go? Was she truly happy ditching her old friends—and her former interests and activities—and hanging out with a new (and questionable) crowd?

While we might not make as radical a change as Taylor appeared to be making—ignoring her old friends, skipping school, and dropping out of positive activities—we can still slip up and make poor life choices.

When we make these choices and then recognize them as mistakes, it's hard to not feel guilty and get mad at ourselves. But instead of beating ourselves up, we can ask God (and others if necessary) to forgive us. God can take our bad feelings about ourselves and use all that negativity to bring about a very positive outcome.

God can always transform bad feelings into something good, which is what happens when He works one of His miraculous interventions.

If someone you love is making some big mistakes, sometimes what that person needs most is an *intervention*. That's what Sarah and Rebekah were planning to do with Taylor. They were going to intervene or step in and try to help her get out of any bad situation she might be headed for.

Interventions are never pleasant, though. The confrontation wasn't going to be fun for Sarah and Rebekah, and it wasn't going to be fun for Taylor either. It is absolutely no fun when we are the one who needs the intervention! Right? It's hard to deal with everything you don't like about yourself and what you're doing wrong and then figure out the ways you need to change. But that's usually the only way to turn things around.

Taylor needed an intervention. Gomer needed an intervention. I need one. We all need one!

Thorns

God provides interventions for those He loves—and that means you and me. He did it for Israel, His beloved people, by allowing them to be oppressed and eventually attacked by their enemies. Doesn't sound very fun, does it? But sometimes interventions come in not-so-pretty packages.

One of these packages might look like a tangle of thorns: "Therefore I will block her path with thornbushes; I will wall her in so she cannot find her way" (Hosea 2:6). Ouch!

In this verse God was telling the Israelites that He would block their way with thorns, enclose them with a wall, and hide their paths. This might sound really weird, but He did this for their own good.

Have you ever gotten tangled up in thorns? You might be able to fight your way through them eventually, but the process sure slows you down, scratches you up, and makes you think twice about how you got there.

Like He did to the Israelites, God sometimes blocks our path of wayward wandering with thorns. It might be prickly, painful conflict we get tangled up in—seriously sharp thorns that God uses to get our attention and show us He has something else in mind for us.

Can you think of a time when you found yourself tangled up in thorns? Maybe it was a relationship with someone—a friend, a parent, a sibling—when conflict always seemed to be happening. You were always arguing, always disagreeing, always pushing each other's buttons.

I know this isn't easy to do, but try to think of that conflict as thorns that are actually helping you slow down and forcing you to think twice about your actions. Let me tell you a story to show you how this works.

One of my friend's daughters—I'll call her Lola for this story—is in constant conflict with her mom. I know this because I recently spent the day with them and heard Mom's version of it in my right ear and Lola's version of it in my left ear!

Now, neither Lola nor her mom is perfect, not by a long shot, but I've got to say poor Lola creates a lot of the drama because of how she interprets her mom's words.

When Mom says, "Lola! You need to turn off your phone. It's 10:00, and the rule is your phone goes off at 10," Lola explodes. "That's not fair!" she shouts. "My friend Grace gets to keep hers on until 10:30!" (Grace is another imaginary name.)

Mom responds, "Well, I'm not Grace's mom. I'm *your* mom—and this is our rule!" (Sound familiar? Grin.)

You can probably imagine what happens next. "You don't trust me!" Lola shouts. "You're trying to control me! I can't stand you! I wish I lived at Grace's house!"

Okay, let's step back and look at this situation. Why is Lola tangled up in thorns? Is it because her phone is supposed to be turned off at 10:00? Is it because she didn't turn it off on time? Is it because her mom told her to turn it off? Is it because Grace has a perfect mother who Lola would be way, way happier living with? Is it because Lola's life would totally transform if she could keep her phone on for an extra 30 minutes every night?

Nope. The thorny tangle happened because of Lola's iddiction. *My way! My wisdom! My wants!*

Lola set up her own sticky situation. She got tangled up in conflict with her mom not because of her iPhone but because of her "I"—in other words, because of her selfishness.

After hearing all the drama, I gently asked Lola to think about the thorny tangle she was constantly finding herself trapped in. "Lola, do you *really* want this?" I asked. "Is it working for you? Is it bringing you peace? Is it making you feel good about yourself?"

Lola pouted, but she saw where I was going. "Nope," she said.

Then we talked about how she could either see that conflict as a dead end in her relationship with her mom, or she could instead let it prevent her from stomping down a path of future unhappiness. The thorny conflict gave Lola a chance to consider where she was heading and decide if she really liked that destination. She didn't, and now she's trying to be more introspective than explosive when it comes to potentially prickly conversations with her mom.

Way to go, Lola!

What about the thorns in your life? Think about how God might be using them as an intervention to keep you from traveling at lightning speed down a path that could destroy you or your relationships.

In fact, please take a moment here to pause with me and pray about this. It's so important! Ask God to give you the grace to thank Him for those thorns and teach you how to detangle when you find yourself stuck in them.

Walls

Hosea said that God would make a barrier to slow down the people He loved: "I will wall her in so that she cannot find her way" (Hosea 2:6).

Do you think God has ever given you a wall that's blocked your way? Forget about slowing down and thinking twice. A wall forces you to come to a screeching stop right where you are! I've had this happen, so I know from experience that it's pretty painful to bang your head against a wall of your own making. But it definitely helps you avoid that path in the future!

Those painful experiences become God's most important interventions in our lives. Sure, they feel like the Great Wall of China when we crash into them. Often they send us sprawling onto a giant mirror that shows us exactly who we are deep inside. And that's usually a reflection we didn't want to see!

We're all dealing with insecurity to some degree, but on the other side of the wall, we can find our security in God. Walls can actually be gifts of love from God to us!

Thorns and walls are never pleasant, but I bet they aren't what come to mind when you think of symbols of love, are they? Not for me! When I think of symbols of love, I think of flowers, dark chocolate, hugs, and kisses—the real kind and the chocolate kind—not thorns and walls!

But the thorns and walls remind us that God sees us, cares about us, and loves us. He loves us so much that He's willing to do whatever it takes to slow us down and draw us back to Himself.

God sometimes throws barriers our way, but He does it out of protection and love for us. I'm sure your parents have done the same thing. Perhaps they've told you, "No, you can't ride in a car with this person," or "No, you can't go to that concert." You might not see it at the time, but they're trying to protect you from a situation that could be dangerous or just not good for you. It's the same way with God. When He plants thorns in your path, consider it a safe turnaround from something dangerous.

Remember, if you find yourself tangled up in thorns or crashing into walls, it might be God showing His love and mercy to you. Think of the thorns and walls as the hands of God pushing against you to turn you toward a better place.

A Better Place

In the New Testament, both James and Peter quote Proverbs 3:34 to tell us more about this. James says, "But he gives us more grace. That is why Scripture says: 'God opposes the proud but shows favor to the humble'" (James 4:6). Peter says the same thing: "All of you, clothe yourselves with humility toward one another, because, 'God opposes the proud but shows favor to the humble'" (1 Peter 5:5).

Think for a minute about the times you've been tangled up in thorns or crashed into walls. Were you acting humble when that happened? I doubt it! For me being humble keeps me going in the right direction. Pride, however, is a terrible GPS! I always end up lost when I follow pride's directions.

Did humility lead my friend's daughter Lola into thorns? Nope! Does humility make us crash into brick walls? No way! God will resist or push back against pride in us because He loves us so much. Now, this doesn't mean that God is *rejecting* you. Sometimes resisting and rejecting can feel like the same thing. But it's actually the opposite. He's resisting you so He can put you in a better place.

Because God is love and He loves perfectly, He lets our paths get choked by thorns. He allows things to trip us up so we'll say, "I need to get back to God. I need to get back to being who He made me to be. I need to remember my real identity!"

> God sees me, values me, and loves me way too much to let me wander off.

So don't resent God if He resists you. It means that He sees you. He values you and loves you way too much to let you wander off. Okay, it's not your favorite gourmet chocolate bar or a stunning bouquet of roses, but God's way is so much better than we could ever imagine when we're tangled up in those thorns.

You probably know from experience that a loving parent disciplines her children because of her affection for them. And she resists or pushes back her children when they're heading down the wrong path. She's not going to let them run wild!

It's like that with God. When our own bad choices are leading us to people, places, or situations that will only bring us harm or pain, He will sometimes stop us right there in our own tracks.

You know that promise that "all things work together for good to them that love God, to them who are called according to his purpose" (Romans 8:28 KJV)? Well, that could mean roadblocks, conflicts, thorns, or walls...all that stuff that God can use for our good.

Invisibility. Insecurity. Identity crisis. Inferiority. Rejection. Every time you've blown up or blown it, God uses *all* of it for your ultimate good!

Can bad things truly be good? Can they actually lead you to something better? Can what feels like resistance from God really be reassurance? Yes!

Sometimes the dissatisfaction that comes from not getting what we want can actually lead us to a deeply satisfying place—the place where God wants us to be.

Facts and Feelings

Think about the times you've been tangled up in thorns or hit a wall. And as you think about those times, ask yourself some questions:

- Why did I feel like I didn't matter?
- Why was I in constant conflict and having so much drama with others?
- Why was I feeling angry?
- Had I received my identity from God, or was I trying to achieve it for myself?
- Was I focused on who God made me, or was I focused on how I wanted Him to make my life change?

- Why did I feel so insecure?
- Did I find my sense of self in what I did or who God made me to be?
- Was I demanding my way, my wants, and my wisdom— or was I content with God's way, His wants, and His wisdom?

That's a pretty intense list of questions, isn't it? Now, don't feel pressured to write down every response or even feel like you *have* to answer everything right away. That would be impossible! But *do* pay attention to the thoughts and feelings that come into your mind. Then ask God to make your feelings work for you and not against you so you can discover the truth.

You can do this by thinking about the facts instead of letting your feelings run the show. That's what my friend's daughter Lola did. The feeling that helped her discover the fact? She was ticked off because her mom made her turn off her phone at 10:00. What was the truth she came away with? She was acting selfish and demanding her own way.

God can help you see your feelings as guides to find the facts, and finding the facts will lead you to the truth.

But before you can find the truth, your heart and mind need to change. How can you change them? By praying truth.

In fact, I have a prayer I pray whenever I find myself in a thorny place or surrounded by walls. I call this special prayer my Faulty Bow Prayer. (Remember the faulty bow from the previous chapter?)

The Faulty Bow Prayer

This prayer is an awesome way to get myself refocused when I'm in a place I don't want to be. If I find myself having conflict with someone, fighting feelings of insecurity, or being tempted to compare myself to others, I pray this prayer. When I do, God helps turn me around and puts me on a better path.

The key word in this prayer is *turn*. Each letter in the word *turn* represents actions God will take to *return* us to Him. The prayer is simple, but powerful: "We turn to You, Lord."

Now, let's get into the heart of the prayer and see what it means to T-U-R-N.

T: Teach Me Your Ways

> Teach me Your way, O LORD; I will walk in Your truth.
>
> Psalm 86:11a NASB

We've talked about the danger of doing things our own way. That's why we need to ask God to teach us *His* way—the way that will never get us into trouble. Because we're human and because we're still learning and growing, we're going to make mistakes and find ourselves doing things our own way. But the more we understand God's way and tell ourselves, *Not my way but Thy way*, the easier it will be to detangle from those thorns or pick ourselves up after we hit the wall.

U: Unite My Heart with Yours

> Unite my heart to fear Your name.
>
> Psalm 86:11b NASB

The second part of this verse instructs us to ask God to unite our hearts to fear, respect, and honor His name and His wisdom. We need to ask God to give us a pure heart. That way we will be focused on Him instead of on ourselves. And it's so much better to be focused on who God is and who He made us to be. So pray, *Focus my heart on You, Lord, honoring Your Name and not my wayward ways.*

R: Restore the Joy of Your Salvation

> Restore to me the joy of Your salvation and sustain me
> with a willing spirit.
>
> Psalm 51:12 NASB

This verse is part of a prayer that King David prayed after he'd gotten tangled up in some treacherous thorns. He was totally in trouble! For starters he'd committed adultery. Then he caused even more trouble by having his mistress's husband murdered. When David took a good, honest look at himself, he saw that his heart was beyond deeply troubled. He was in total agony! And he'd lost his joy—not his salvation, but his joy. He needed God to create a clean heart in him and restore his joy.

When you find yourself scratched up by thorns or banged up from hitting the wall too many times, you need your joy restored too. God always returns us to Himself through forgiveness, but we also need to ask Him to reinstall our joy. And He always will! We find joy when we get back to Him because in His presence is "fullness of joy" (Psalm 16:11 NASB).

N: Never Leave Me or Forsake Me

> For He Himself has said, "I will never desert you, nor
> will I ever forsake you."
>
> Hebrews 13:5 NASB

God has promised that He will never leave us or forsake us. So when we pray, *Never leave me*, we aren't asking Him to do something that He wouldn't ever do. We're just reminding Him, and ourselves, of our own need for His presence. He'll never, ever leave you—*ever*!

When you talk to God and turn back to Him, you'll find Him waiting right there for you even in your thorniest place. Can you remember a time when He was tangled in thorns for you? When He hung on a cross and wore those thorns as a crown? He did that so you would never, ever have to be tangled in thorns and injured by them.

Romans 8:29 gives us a good idea of why God lovingly lets us get tangled up in thorns and run into walls: "For those God foreknew he also predestined to be conformed to the image of his Son."

Sweet girl, if you belong to Christ, God has a personal commitment to keep you on His path even if that means you'll bang into walls and get tangled up in thorns every now and then.

If you spend your life pursuing self, you'll only become more insecure. If you live your life striving to be seen and noticed, you'll just feel that much more invisible. If you dedicate your days to selfishly going after everything you want, you won't find happiness. You'll just find exhaustion and probably depression.

> When I focus on God,
> I won't feel invisible.

But when you see what God can do in your life and you focus on Him, you'll be thankful for all the times He intervenes, picks you up, dusts you off, and places you gently and lovingly back on the path to living a life of purpose and joy—a life lived for Him.

God not only *loves me* and wants me to *return to Him,* but He goes to *great lengths* to get me *back.*

#TheInvisibleBook

#heart

The place where your treasure is, is the place
you will most want to be, and end up being.
—LUKE 12:34 MSG

Emma thought to herself, *Running for student body office really isn't*
my thing, but it would look so good on my college application. I hate
public speaking, and I really don't have time to add another activity to
my schedule, but I'm going to do it anyway.

It was the spring of Emma's junior year of high school, and she
had college on the brain. Emma was the youngest of five kids. Her
older siblings had all attended or were currently attending really
good colleges. In high school they had easily achieved stellar grades,
nearly perfect SAT scores, and tons of leadership roles in addition
to enjoying major musical and athletic talents.

Emma was different, though. She loved art, but she'd quit paint-
ing lessons because her AP math and science classes were so difficult
and demanding. She loved writing poetry on her blog, but softball
practices and oboe lessons took up so much time after school that
she hadn't had time to write a blog post in months. Truth be told,

she didn't love softball, and she wasn't that good at it anyway. And music? Emma really wanted to play the guitar, but she'd chosen to play the oboe because it was a challenging instrument that would look good on her college applications.

Her best friend, Carly, was always trying to get Emma to go to youth group and volunteer with her at the homeless teen shelter (one of Emma's favorite things to do), but Carly didn't have the pressure Emma had at home. And while Emma's parents didn't flat-out tell her she needed to be a success like her older brothers and sisters, Emma felt the pressure big-time.

My life right now isn't really my choice, Emma told herself. *Once I'm in college, I can do the things I want to do. I just need to do what I can to get there!*

⁓⸻⁓

Emma's situation is a pretty typical one for lots of teenagers. She thought she knew who she was and what she wanted, but when she started thinking things through, Emma realized that she didn't really know who she was or what she wanted out of life—or more importantly, what God wanted out of her life.

Her problem wasn't her busy schedule or her conflicted emotions. Her problem was her relationship with herself. She'd set up a false idol of accomplishment, and she was going to do whatever it took to serve it.

Emma probably felt a lot of pressure to achieve. With those amazing siblings, how could she feel otherwise? But like all of us, Emma was struggling with iddiction. And her iddiction had morphed into idolatry.

Emma had become her own idol, her own god, and a perfect college application was what she was using to serve herself. She hadn't wanted to feel invisible, especially compared to all her super siblings, and so she learned to find security and satisfaction in a sparkling list of accomplishments—even if they weren't things she actually enjoyed!

Emma had decided she was going to do the things that looked impressive on paper, no matter if she was gifted at them or not. Just like Gomer, she'd made up her mind to go her own way.

Isn't that the way it always happens? It's hard to tell when something good—like challenging ourselves with hard classes or being driven to do our best—begins to become a god thing, but it's easy to see that it all begins with "I."

Becoming Your Own Idol

It's kind of strange to think about becoming your own idol, but it always happens when we keep our focus on ourselves instead of on God and other people. Right now we're going to return to Gomer's story to understand how this whole idol thing works. By sneaking into Gomer's thought bubble to see what she was thinking, we're going to discover how "I" can become your own idol. And we're going to spell out *idol* three different ways, using three different acronyms to help us understand this way of thinking.

Idol #1: I Desire Other Lovers

Gomer was pretty much controlled by her desires. She wanted more than what she had. Maybe she thought that what she had wasn't enough or she'd be more satisfied with a different life.

Remember Emma at the beginning of this chapter? She'd gotten caught up in what she thought she wanted—a superlong list of activities, perfect grades, admission into a prestigious college—and ignored her real talents and gifts in art, poetry, playing guitar, and helping other people. Whenever she felt scared or frustrated, she just added another activity to her growing list of commitments.

It's easy to feel like we'll be invisible if we don't get what we want. Our "other lovers" can be things like accomplishments, popularity, material possessions, or a perfect appearance. When we become our own idol, it's because of desire—a desire for things to be exactly the way we want them.

Idol #2: I Don't Obey the Lord

We've learned through Gomer's story that wandering thoughts eventually lead to wandering feet. Her desires for other lovers and another life led to disobedience. She had promised to be faithful to Hosea and her family, but her desire for a different life was stronger than her desire to do what was right. So she stepped out.

We become our own idol when we start—and then continue— to disobey God. Instead of listening to what He wants us to do with our lives, we go our own way. We forget to read our Bibles and spend time with God. We put off going to youth group because we're too busy. We stop thinking about how God wants us to treat other people and focus only on how we want to be treated. And then we find ourselves in a place we never wanted to be.

Idol #3: I Disregard His Offer of Love

Gomer didn't admit that all the good things she had—even after she left Hosea—were from and because of Hosea. The silver and gold, wool and flax, and oil and drink (remember that stuff?) she had were all from Hosea, but she let it all go and disregarded it.

Our worth and satisfaction will always be found in God, but we go to other things—friends, social media, shopping—to find what we think we're missing. Then we give credit to these things for bringing us happiness, entertainment, and stress relief. And that, of course, means we go right back to these same things when we're feeling needy!

Look back at these three IDOL acronyms, and you can see it's a three-step process. First, we *desire* other lovers. Next, we *don't obey the Lord*. And finally, we *disregard* His offer of love. What do each of these steps have in common?

I-D-O-L

The first letter of *idol* is *I*. All idolatry is the result of loving ourselves, loving "I." We become our own idol when we love and serve ourselves more than we love and serve God. That's what Gomer did. She went for other lovers and used them to serve herself. These other lovers weren't the idols. They are what I call *idolotrinkets*.

When we feel invisible or insecure, we can use good things— like activities, friendships, or clothes—as sources of satisfaction and even self-worship. That's how these good things become idolotrinkets—little idols in our lives that take the place of God and all the good He has planned for us.

Fun, friendships, and fashion aren't wrong, but the importance you attach to them or the way you use them to serve yourself *can* be wrong.

The main problem for Gomer—and for you and me—is that we are iddicts who easily become our own idols. We use anything that captures our attention to satisfy us, please us, and boost our self-worth.

This isn't a new idea. People have done this since the beginning of time! We're all idol-makers if we're given the right conditions. That's what we iddicts do. We make idolotrinkets. We take good things and make them god things.

So let's dig a little deeper and figure out how we can identify our idolotrinkets.

Clues

You might have just one or two idolotrinkets in your life or an entire charm bracelet full! Or you might not be sure what exactly has become an idolotrinket in your life. If that's the case, pay close attention because we're going to figure this out!

Our goal is to find out who we really are—who God created us to be. In order to do this, we need to get rid of the things that feed our pride or give us a false sense of identity and security. So we're going to pause, pray, and ask God to guide us as we discover the six clues that identify our idolotrinkets.

Anything I use to *complete* God will *compete* with God.

Clue #1: Desire

Spend a moment thinking about what you want—what you really, really want! Think about what you want so badly that you can't imagine not having it. It might be something you already have and feel scared when you imagine losing it.

This might be hard, so think about the things I've listed below and ask yourself: *If I had to choose between faithfulness to Jesus and that person or thing, would it be a hard choice to make?*

- Friendships
- Acceptance
- Reputation
- Identity
- Appearance

Now ask yourself: *Is something that I desire creating an idol that's guiding the things I do, the words I say, and the way I act?* If you can't live without it, it's probably an idolotrinket.

Clue #2: Dwell

What do you spend a lot of your time thinking about? What do you think about all the time? It's not so much daydreaming about how much you love or want it, it's more like you obsess about how to get it or what it would be like if you didn't have it. (If you're not sure, look at your social media pictures and postings. That will probably give you a clue!)

Whatever we think about the most is basically serving as our god. And if we are always on our own minds, well that's it! See how easy it is for you to turn into your own idol? When your thoughts automatically turn toward the people, situations, and things that please, affirm, and build up your self-worth, those are your idolotrinkets.

Clue #3: Defend

If someone questions something that you have, want, or do, are you offended? Do their questions make you feel threatened or defensive? Do you feel like you have to make excuses for or defend your obsession?

Most of us are guilty of justifying our actions with thoughts like these: *What I'm doing isn't so bad—other people do way worse things!*

Everybody else does it, so why should I be any different? I totally deserve this, so I'm going to do it no matter what!

If you have to rationalize your behavior with those kinds of thoughts, you're probably protecting an idolotrinket.

Clue #4: Dedicate

What do you love to do? What seems to be a part of you? Dedication can be a really great thing, but it becomes a problem when you do anything possible to find a way to make something happen—especially if you're relying on secrecy or sacrifice to make it happen.

Staying up way too late on social media, borrowing money from your parents (and then forgetting to return it), hiding what you're reading or watching, deleting text messages you don't want your parents to read—if you're dabbling in this kind of secretive behavior, you're probably dealing with an idolotrinket.

Clue #5: Deny

Here's another question to ask yourself: *Have I ever denied what I'm doing, thinking about, or wanting?* If you're afraid that others will find out what you're spending your time, your thoughts, or your money on, that indicates an idolotrinket.

We won't hide something if we don't have anything to hide. So if you're hiding something, it's probably an idolotrinket. Ask God to open your eyes and show you the things you're hiding, especially habits you know you need to break, like an addiction to social media, an obsession with gossip, or a desire to watch movies or TV shows that don't have the best values. Definitely pray about these things. It takes time to break negative habits and replace them with positive ones. But if you rely on God and are patient with yourself, you can do it!

Clue #6: Depend

Is there anything you find yourself depending on to make you feel complete, or are you okay with who you are?

If you find that you need something other than God to complete you, like a boyfriend or a certain social standing so you can fit in, it looks like you've found another idolotrinket.

So what do you think? Were you able to identify any idolotrinkets? If you have, welcome to my world...to all of our worlds! And don't be discouraged if you've realized that you've become your own idol. Don't get down on yourself if you realize you've been using idolotrinkets to serve the idol of "I." God can turn things around for you!

Instead of freaking out about the idolotrinkets in your life or just saying whatever to them and continuing on your not-so-merry path, ask God to use those idolotrinkets as reminders. They're reminders of how we need to look to God for satisfaction instead of to ourselves.

Remember, those objects of our affection—like movies or music or fashion—are not bad things in and of themselves, but they *can* become idolotrinkets if they're used in the wrong way.

When you think you've found an idolotrinket, ask yourself, *Is the way I'm treating this object serving myself or honoring God?*

You'll probably know the answer! And if you don't know it right away, God will show you if you're using that thing, desire, longing, or object to serve yourself or to honor Him. Then ask Him to give you the grace and power to honor Him.

It will happen. It will turn out okay! God honors the girl who honors Him: "For those who honor Me I will honor, and those who despise me will be lightly esteemed" (1 Samuel 2:30 NASB).

If you despise something, that means you don't have any regard for it. You don't think much of it at all. When we replace the things God made for us and the desires He gave us with our own agenda and ideas, we despise God. Sounds pretty harsh, but that's the truth. It's never a good idea to take something God made to glorify Himself and remake it into something we use to serve our own selves.

Just so you don't get lost in the world of ideas here, let's look at some practical examples.

- If your idolotrinket is approval from others (which could be the approval of friends, teachers, parents, or coaches), ask yourself: *Am I looking for approval from others to feed my own sense of accomplishment, or do I want their approval because God will receive honor if others approve of me?*

- If your idolotrinket is popularity, ask yourself: *Am I trying to be popular to make myself more important, or am I seeking popularity because if I'm popular, God will be honored?*

- If your idolotrinket is acceptance, ask yourself: *Does trying hard for acceptance serve to make me more significant, or do I try to be accepted because if I'm accepted by others, God will be honored?*

- If your idolotrinket is social media, ask yourself: *Am I spending my free time online to try to serve my own needs, or am I spending time on social media to bring honor to God?*

- If your idolotrinket is your appearance, ask yourself: *Am I trying to look (fashionable, cute, preppy, trendy, or whatever look you're going for) to serve my own sense of identity, or am I dressing like this because my goal is to honor God?*

- If your idolotrinket is good grades and success, ask yourself: *Am I wanting to get straight A's and succeed because those things will make me feel better about myself, or am I wanting to do my best because it honors God?*

- If your idolotrinket is material things (a car, the latest smartphone, brand-name jewelry, or makeup), ask yourself: *Am I using the things I have or the things I want to serve my own needs, or am I using them to honor God?*

- If your idolotrinket is pleasure, ask yourself: *Am I wanting these things (gourmet coffee drinks, parties, fun outings, or vacations) to bring me pleasure because it serves me or because by enjoying those things, God is honored too?*

As you reflect on your possible idolotrinkets and ask yourself these questions, God will reveal the state of your heart, and you'll also discover His heart for you.

Now, here's the thing. Sometimes God may nudge your heart and let you know that it's not dishonoring Him to spend time on social media, work hard to accomplish something, or spend money on a fancy coffee drink (and buy one for a friend while you're at it!). Working hard, having fun, and enjoying life are all very good things if we keep our hearts in the right place.

It's not about your habits. It's about your heart! But your habits reflect your heart. That's why it's so important to look at your habits—so you can see your heart more clearly.

God tells us that where we find our treasure, we'll also find our heart (see Luke 12:34). When God is our treasure, our hearts will be drawn toward Him. We'll focus on honoring Him. When we keep thinking only of ourselves, though, *we* become our own treasure and use our idolotrinkets only to make ourselves happy.

> When God is my treasure,
> my heart will be drawn toward Him.

Now, there will be times when fulfilling your desires *does* honor God. But there are also times when going for what you want might serve yourself without bringing any honor to God. Then there are also times when you can serve yourself and honor God all at the same time.

The key is knowing the difference, and it takes practice to figure this out. It's the condition of your heart that's important. If you're struggling with this—and it makes sense that you would be because adults struggle with the exact same thing—talk to a parent, a youth leader, or another mentor about it. Ask them to pray with you about seeing your heart.

God wants you to have deep and lasting satisfaction and an unshakable identity. He wants you to feel good about yourself! He wants you to rest in His love for you. He wants you to know that this inner confidence and security can only come from Him. He is the giver of all good things!

You might feel invisible because you're looking for yourself in the eyes of an idolotrinket who can't see you, care about you, or give you what you're longing for. So let's just stop looking for yourself that way, okay? Go ahead and identify those idolotrinkets, and then put them down and walk away because there's only one God—the true God—who satisfies.

> I'm still your GOD, the God who saved you out of
> Egypt. I'm the only real God you've ever known.
>
> Hosea 13:4 MSG

When you find yourself spinning your wheels and stuck trying to meet your own needs, stop and go to God. Ask Him to place His desires in your heart. Ask Him to switch your focus away from yourself and to Him and others. Ask Him to reveal the gifts and longings He's placed in you—things that will honor Him and help you become the awesome girl of God He created you to be.

And then thank Him for being the giver of all good things!

#covered

We can be so sure that every detail in our lives
of love for God is worked into something good.
— ROMANS 8:28 MSG

Morgan thought, *This is terrible. I thought I could trust Ella! Now everyone is going to hate me!*

What had started out as an innocent texting conversation between Morgan and her best friend had turned into a nightmare when Ella shared their lighthearted comments with some other kids who shared the comments with other kids and so on until practically everyone in the entire school knew about the conversation.

Ella was always joking around, so at first Morgan had assumed this was one of their typical just-for-fun conversations. True, they'd made fun of a few kids and some teachers. But they were only kidding! And in the past, Ella had kept their conversations private. But not this time.

For some reason Ella had decided to share Morgan's comments (while deleting her own, of course!) with, well, more people than Morgan cared to imagine. Now the whole school knew that Morgan thought that Jessica's makeup made her look like a circus clown, Max was the most arrogant jerk she'd ever met, and Mrs. Johnson looked like a zombie.

I totally trusted Ella, Morgan thought. *How could she do this to me? And how am I ever going to go back to school on Monday and face all those people? I so wish I could go back and redo that conversation!*

Morgan slid her phone into her desk drawer (after silencing it so she couldn't hear any message notifications) and opened her math book. Maybe studying would take her mind off herself and what others must have been saying about her right now. But it was impossible to concentrate. She was the only thing on her mind, and she was certain that's what everyone else was thinking about too!

·⁓⟋⟋⟍⟍⟋⟍⟍⟍⟍⟍~·

It may have started way back in 2003 with the social network MySpace, or maybe it happens because every time we switch on our computer screens, we see words on the desktop like *my* documents, *my* music, and *my* downloads. I'm pretty sure that iPhones, iPads, iPods, and iMacs reinforce it. (Notice what letter each of these products starts with?) Yep, we are a world totally obsessed with me, myself, and I!

And like Morgan we can be on our own minds a lot! There's a reason idol begins with an *I*. When we're always thinking about ourselves, we become *iddicts*. And then we head straight for idolatry, and it just gets worse from there.

How Did You Get Here?

Remember Gomer? She was another girl who made some poor choices based on how she felt at the moment and what she thought she wanted. She left the love of her life, Hosea, and her kids and went back to her wild ways. But now her luck has run out. Nobody's interested in Gomer anymore. What was once new and exciting is now old news.

Once showered with diamonds, Gomer has now been stripped of her dignity. Pursued and then discarded time and time again, Gomer has grown weathered and worn. As her allure and attractiveness have faded, Gomer has grown desperate. Hosea's once beloved bride is now selling her body to pay for her own bread and water, wool and flax, and oil and drink.

Yes, Gomer has fallen about as low as she can go. And this is where she's landed. She's standing on a slave block waiting to be sold. Just one of several slaves being auctioned off to the highest bidder at the local slave market, Gomer must have this one thought running through her mind: *How in the world did I get here?*

We don't know exactly how Gomer wound up on that slave block, but we do know she was no longer a carefree social butterfly. The party had ended. She'd gone from dazzling to disgraced. Her own choices led to her chains.

When we forget about God and focus on ourselves and our idolotrinkets, we always end up paying a huge price. Maybe we don't end up standing on a slave block, but we do find ourselves stuck in places we don't want to be and feeling guilty about how we got there. It's like Morgan and her carefree texting conversation. She didn't stop to consider the people she was making fun of. She didn't ask herself, *What would Jesus say if He saw my conversation?* She just went with what she wanted and found herself in a place she didn't want to be.

When we make a few small choices that take us a few steps in the wrong direction, those choices add up to become the chains in our lives.

Here's how it works. When a girl's idolotrinket is *acceptance*—the "please, please like me" syndrome—her slave master will be *insecurity* because she's controlled by the fear of not performing well and not doing exactly what everyone else wants her to do. She'll live her life wondering if she's good enough and if she's all that others expect her to be.

What about a girl whose idolotrinket is *significance*—the "please approve of me" syndrome? Her slave master will be an *identity crisis* because she'll always be striving to be somebody, to matter, to earn affection and identity. She'll never be able to be happy with who she is because she doesn't even *know* who she is. And because there will always be someone who seems more significant than her, she'll constantly wonder who she is.

And then there's the girl with the idolotrinket of *pleasure*—the "please give me more" syndrome. That girl's slave master will be *discontentment* because she'll always need and want more—more stuff, more fun, more friends. Because there will always be more to need and want, she'll never be content. Likewise, someone else will always have something more or something better. Talk about never being satisfied with what you already have!

Do you recognize any of these idolotrinkets? Do you see yourself in any of those girls? Have you ever been in any of those situations?

Stumbling Along

It should be pretty obvious by now that Gomer wasn't the only girl in history who was enslaved by her sins and chained up by her own choices. Even if our bad choices were different from Gomer's, we've all felt swallowed up by invisibility, and we've all gone wandering off alone into insignificance. We've felt like we don't matter and that nobody sees us. Or, like Morgan, we suddenly realize that we wish nobody *would* see us!

Maybe you've recently done something you regret—gotten in

a fight with a friend, spread some rumors, didn't tell your parents the truth. When this happens, we struggle to accept ourselves, and we struggle to accept God's forgiveness. Sometimes we feel so badly about ourselves, we can't imagine God looking at us with love ever again! And we think if God doesn't love us, how could anyone else even like us?

When we blow it, it's super easy to beat ourselves up.

Now, here's something really important. Sometimes we get to this point as a result of our own bad choices or a heart that's strayed from God. But sometimes we can't really see any actions that got us wrapped up in chains. We've simply found ourselves living out our humanity and struggling with our own weaknesses.

Sometimes you can feel like you're the only one who ever messes up. But everyone is going to stumble and make mistakes. We just can't help it. It's a part of being human! So we shouldn't feel ashamed when we mess up. Yes, we should take a look at what we're doing and ask God—and others if necessary—for forgiveness, but beating ourselves up isn't going to get us anywhere.

When we're caught in chains of sin or selfishness, it's pretty common to feel like we're the only one in that situation. But sometimes we're caught there because we're simply being human. We're always going to stumble and make mistakes, and this makes us feel ashamed, like we shouldn't be so weak or clueless. I know it makes no sense at all, but it's still so real.

I remember one night when I was in college, I needed someone to walk me from the student center back to my dorm. (Remember, I'm blind!) Even though I use a white cane to help me navigate, I do a lot better when I can actually hold onto someone's arm. But back in my college days, I didn't carry my cane everywhere I went.

On this particular night, none of my usual friends were around, and I was starting to stress out. *Who will walk me to my dorm?* I wondered. *I don't think I can get there alone!* While I was trying to push back my inner panic, another student approached me to ask me a question. *Thank You, God!* I whispered to myself.

I didn't know Chelsie well, but I knew her well enough to swallow my pride and ask her to walk me back to my dorm. Now, please know that I was a ton more self-conscious about my blindness back then! I was painfully self-aware, and all I wanted was to be normal and fit in. I never wanted to be needy. So asking Chelsie to walk with me was a pretty big deal.

Because I didn't have my cane with me that night, I was totally dependent on Chelsie's prompts to step up or down and do whatever else to keep me from falling flat on my face.

Chelsie, though, had absolutely no experience helping a blind girl navigate the campus. And because I didn't want to make a big deal about my blindness, I didn't bother to tell her how she could help me. #notsmart

You can imagine how great this was going to go! As we walked I held Chelsie's elbow, tried to pay close attention to where we were, and counted my steps to the curb. I thought I knew the campus pretty well, but I was wrong. When I got to the first curb, I stepped—sort of! What I actually did was stagger and step down really hard.

"Oh!" Chelsie exclaimed in surprise.

"It's okay." I tried to make light of the situation before promptly jamming my toe into the next curb.

"Oh!" Chelsie responded again.

"It's okay," I replied.

This went on for a while until I stumbled as I stepped from the street to the sidewalk. But this time instead of Chelsie saying, "Oh!" and me saying, "It's okay," I blurted out, "I'm sorry!"

I'm sorry? I wondered. *That was a dumb thing to say! Why did I say that?*

And then Chelsie responded in a happy tone, "It's okay!" Talk about a crazy moment!

I still think about my walk with Chelsie. Why did I feel like I had to apologize? I felt ashamed because I couldn't figure out the steps on my own, but there was absolutely no reason for me to feel ashamed or tell her, "I'm sorry." I was a young college student who was blind, for heaven's sake! And sweet Chelsie was a college freshman who didn't know what else to do. Neither of us had done anything wrong. We were simply two young women living out our less-than-perfect humanity. And because of this, I felt I needed to apologize for who I was and for the mistakes I was making, even though none of it was my fault!

That's just how life goes. We make mistakes. We forget things. We let friends down. We let our rooms get messy. We're impatient with our parents and our siblings. And when we find ourselves acting like the flawed human beings we are, we forget our identity as loved, accepted, and amazing girls of God and start to scramble for identity!

And while we're trying to get ourselves unstuck and unchained, we keep hearing little lies: *You're the only girl who can't make her life work. Everyone else is perfect. You're the only one who keeps messing up. Nobody else has a problem with that.*

When we find ourselves caught being human, we feel like our low self-esteem, perfectionism, and feelings of guilt or regret are on display for everyone to see. And our instinct is to hide—to isolate ourselves—because we just *know* we're all alone in this mess.

Girl, don't hide! You're so not the only one! *Everyone* sins. *Everyone* stumbles. *Everyone* messes up. *Everyone* struggles.

But *everyone* is also loved—and accepted. So don't feel like you need to hide. You might have made some mistakes and be stuck in a place you don't want to be, but God doesn't identify you based on where you are. He identifies you based on *who* you are and *Whose* you are. You are His! So if you feel like you need to hide, instead run to Him and hide in Him.

God's Love Covers You

Think about how you feel when you just don't want to face something—a big test, someone who has bullied you, telling someone no. What do you usually want to do instead? Remember how Morgan wanted to make herself disappear after she realized everyone knew what she'd been saying about them? She hid her phone in a drawer, and you know that hiding your phone—which connects you to everyone you know—means you want to hide yourself!

Hide. That's what most of us want to do. When I mess up or don't want to deal with something, I want to go hide in my closet or go back to bed and hide under the covers! But I'm not a little kid anymore, so I can't hide under the covers…or can I? Actually, I can—and you can too! We can hide under the cover of God's perfect love.

So the next time you feel like you don't want to face something, instead of hiding behind excuses, a fake personality, or the false security of an idolotrinket, hide under the cover of God's acceptance and love.

> Keep me as the apple of your eye; hide me in the shadow
> of your wings.
>
> Psalm 17:8

If you don't remember anything else from this book, remember this: Jesus loves you. If you remember that, you'll always end up okay! When you remember that Jesus loves you, you remember that someone is always there for you. When you remember that Jesus loves you, you remember that what other people think of you doesn't matter. What He thinks of you is what counts. When you remember that Jesus loves you, you remember that it's okay to make mistakes because in His grace and forgiveness, He's there to pick you up, dust you off, and put you back on your feet.

So don't be so hard on yourself! Don't feel like you have to hide under the covers or shut yourself away in your room. Don't let your mistakes and your mess-ups define who you are.

Can you imagine the emotions Gomer must have felt as she stood all alone on that slave block waiting to be sold? She had no clue who was going to buy her or where her new home would be or what her new owner was going to make her do. I'd feel pretty scared in that situation, wouldn't you?

Standing there in chains, Gomer must have been saying to herself, *Girl, you totally blew it! You are beyond hope. Nothing good is ever going to happen to you again.*

The Bible describes Gomer in these pretty depressing terms: "swallowed up...wandering alone...like something no one wanted...who had sold herself."

Those phrases sound pretty grim, but Gomer was still wanted by God. His love for her and Hosea's love for her never, ever wavered. No matter what she did, no matter where she went, she was never, ever alone.

It's the same for you. No matter what you do or where you go, you're never alone. And God's love for you will never, ever waver.

God doesn't want you to feel all alone. He wants you to rest in His love and forgiveness. He doesn't want you to set out all by yourself and wander away from Him. He wants you to always be with Him. He doesn't want you to believe the lie that nobody wants to be your friend or hang out with you. He wants you to believe the truth that you are loved and valued by Him.

God can always take what seems like a dead end and make a

pathway to freedom. He can always take you from your lowest point and turn it into one of your best memories ever.

> God can always take what seems like a
> dead end and make a pathway to freedom.

The Best Thing and the Worst Thing

Have you ever experienced a time or a place that had some of your best memories *and* some of your worst memories all wrapped up in one?

Maybe it was your kindergarten classroom. Maybe your teacher was super strict and never smiled and you missed your mom and your younger brother more than you could have imagined. While you were lining up to go to recess and feeling so alone, you knew they were at home reading picture books and drinking steaming cups of hot cocoa with marshmallows. But then you met your best friend, and the two of you spent many happy recesses together pretending you were ponies and making some of your best memories ever! #itcouldhappen

Or maybe it was that season you played volleyball. First you dislocated your wrist and then you sprained your ankle and when you finally returned to the court, you got hit in the head with the ball and had to sit out the rest of that game. While you'd never want to hold onto the injuries, you've kept all the get-well cards your coach and teammates made for you. And you can smile when you remember how they were always there to hold doors open and make things easier when you were hobbling around on crutches. Your best memories and your worst memories all in the same place!

Or to make it really simple, it could be like your favorite energy bar. You love it because of the chocolate, but you hate it because of the cashews. The best thing and the worst thing all wrapped up in the same package!

In life nothing's going to be perfect. The bitter will always accompany the sweet. We'll always have triumphs, and we'll always have troubles. We walk in faith for a while, and then we wander off into unfaithfulness. It happens to all of us.

But God can always take the lowest point in your life—the time when you made an honest mistake, the time when you used really poor judgment, the time when you spoke something or wrote something without considering the cost of your words—and create some of your best memories from it.

You'll remember the time your mom hugged you even though you deserved punishment. You'll remember the time your teacher let you try again even though you failed the first time. You'll remember the time your friend said "I forgive you" even though you said some nasty things about her.

And most of all, I hope you remember all the times God hugged you, let you try again, said "I forgive you," and then removed your chains, took your hand, and turned you back to Him.

I may be *perfectly imperfect,* but I am a *loved, accepted, and amazing* girl of God.

#TheInvisibleBook

#future

*I know what I'm doing. I have it all planned
out—plans to take care of you, not abandon
you, plans to give you the future you hope for.*
—JEREMIAH 29:11 MSG

Mallory scrunched down further in her seat, willing her history teacher to somehow skip her. Maybe she'd lost Mallory's test! Maybe she had gotten the papers mixed up and another student had gotten credit for Mallory's score—and vice versa.

She'd known for weeks that the history final was looming, but it seemed that Mallory was always too busy to study. At gymnastics practice, they'd run late to prepare for a big meet. Then her grandparents came all the way from Florida to visit. And there were always little assignments to catch up on—vocab quizzes for French, the usual math homework, science labs to write up. Studying for the history final always seemed to be the last thing on her to-do list—the item that never got checked off or crossed out.

The night before the test, Mallory tried to cram, but it was just too much. The names, the dates, the places—she couldn't memorize it all, and so she slammed her book shut in frustration, stuck a bag of popcorn in the microwave, and turned on her favorite TV program. If she couldn't study for the final, maybe she could at least forget about it!

Deep down Mallory knew what was coming...a great big fail!

And sure enough, there it was on paper: an F with the message, "Please see me after class."

Great. Just great.

But when Mallory stood slouched in front of her teacher's desk after class, she received the surprise of her life.

"Mallory, I know this isn't up to your usual standards," her teacher said. "You've had plenty of time to prepare for this test."

"I know," Mallory said with a shrug, her eyes downcast.

"I'm going to do something I don't usually do," said her teacher, tapping the test with the tip of her pencil. "I'm going to give you another chance. You may have one week to study, and I'll give you another test next week."

Seriously? Mallory looked up at the teacher. She couldn't speak! Another chance? When she clearly hadn't put in the effort? Was her teacher serious?

As if reading Mallory's mind, her history teacher smiled. "Yes, I'm serious. Now go home and study!"

"Thank you!" Mallory gasped. "I'm going to study harder this week than I've ever studied before!"

·~~~~~~·

Before her teacher gave her a second chance, Mallory just wanted to disappear or, rather, she wanted her history test to disappear. She was ashamed of her performance on the test. To make things worse, she knew it was her own fault for not studying.

Have you ever been in a situation like that? You feel hopeless. You know you've failed. You can't see any good way out of it or, to be honest, any bad way out of it for that matter!

Our girl, Gomer, was in that very situation as she stood up on the slave block. How was she going to get out of this one? Could anything good come out of her current situation?

If cellphones had existed back in Gomer's day, I can guarantee you the towers would have been overloaded the day Gomer went up for sale. Everyone—and I mean E-V-E-R-Y-O-N-E—would have been on the phone!

Did you hear about Gomer? Do you think Hosea knows she's being sold? What do you think he'll do when he finds out?

But it actually would have been old news to Hosea because he'd already found out from God Himself. God called on him to redeem Gomer—to give her a second chance. He told the heart-broken guy, "Go, show your love to your wife again, though she is loved by another" (Hosea 3:1).

It's important to think about what God *didn't* say here. He didn't say, "Go, judge your wife and be really harsh on her while you're at it!" He didn't say, "Go, show Gomer how disappointed you are in her and really make her cry!"

God told Hosea to show love, not harshness or disappointment. Love!

Hosea had suffered the ultimate rejection—rejection by his beloved wife—and now God was telling him to do the unthinkable. He was supposed to buy back Gomer *and* love her again.

Wow!

We've been trying to see ourselves in Gomer, but think about it from Hosea's perspective for a second. How would you feel if you were him? How right was it that he was expected to spend his own hard-earned money to buy back Gomer and then keep treating her with love and respect, especially when she had been so disrespectful to him?

So, how did Hosea actually manage to do this? He did it by loving God more than he loved Gomer—by loving God more than he loved himself.

Hosea *had* to feel hurt by Gomer's actions. He had to feel disgusted with how she'd been acting. He had to feel embarrassed at his situation. But Hosea had been called by God, so he followed God. And his willingness to obey probably gave him the strength to obey. Deep down the romantic in me hopes—really hopes—that he still loved her. Don't you?

Even if he still did love her, though, was it fair of God to ask Hosea to do such a crazy thing? Gomer sure didn't deserve to be saved, did she? She deserved to be left on that slave block alone to think about her mistakes and her failures.

But Hosea—and God—gave Gomer a second chance. She was allowed to retake the test, so to speak. They wiped out her failing grade and told her to return to her studies and try again.

God doesn't come to our rescue because we deserve it. He rescues us because He is merciful and loving. Saving us is who He is and what He does.

I am not loved because I'm worthy.
I am loved because God thinks
I'm worth it!

Valuable

Hosea didn't buy back Gomer because she was worthy, but because she was worth it. So he went to the slave block with money in hand—the equivalent of about 30 pieces of silver that he'd had to scrape together (along with some random grain called barley).

I can imagine Hosea having just drained his savings account and arriving at the market where the slave auction was being held. His heart must have been crushed to see the woman he loved standing there in her tattered clothing for all the crowd to see.

When the auctioneer opened the bidding, Hosea offered the first bid. Another bid was made, and Hosea upped his price. The bidding went on until Hosea offered his 30 pieces of silver. The auctioneer's hammer fell, and Gomer was pronounced, "Sold!"

Glancing up to see who would be her new master, Gomer must have cried tears of shame and relief and regret and uncertainty when she saw who had bought her. She must have thought, *Will he ever forgive me? Can he ever accept me? How can he ever love me again?*

As Gomer was thinking these things, Hosea made his way to the front of the room, gave the auctioneer a pouch of silver coins, and pointed to a heaping bag of barley sitting on the auction house floor. The auctioneer nodded, shoved the coins in his pocket, and pulled out a key. Then with one swift motion, he unlocked the chain. As it clattered to the floor, Hosea reached for Gomer. Yet she could not look into his eyes.

Lifting her dirty hand, Hosea brought it to his lips and kissed it. He then walked his wife off the slave block while covering her with his cloak and whispering to her, "Come back home with me where you belong. You will not be a slave anymore. You will be my wife again."

Gomer was safe again. Loved again. Valuable again.

If you're trapped in insecurity, God whispers, *You are safe in Me.*

If you're stuck in an identity crisis, God says, *You are found in Me.*

If you're feeling frustrated, discontent, or just flat-out depressed and angry, God is still there for you!

No matter where you are or what you're dealing with, God sees you. And He will meet you right where you are.

Chains or Change

Even after she'd been set free, Gomer must have remembered what those heavy chains felt like. Her before and after pictures (think of the kind you see in magazines) were pretty clear—once in chains, now free from chains.

Our chains are just as gone as Gomer's were, but because we can't see them, we forget they're not on us anymore. Because of this, we sometimes think we still have them on, and so I'm going to give you a creative way to think about your chains—you know, the ones you *used* to wear!

Think of your chains as Post-it notes, not superglue! You know the difference, right? A Post-it note sticks to your notebook, mirror, or textbooks pretty well, doesn't it? It stays there until you remove it. If that little piece of paper were stuck to the same place with superglue, though, what would happen when you tried to take it off? You'd tug and tug, but it wouldn't come completely off.

When God saves you, He sets you free. The sin you thought was superglued to your soul becomes a Post-it note. God peels it away and frees you from it. You no longer feel like you're nobody, like you don't matter or like you're invisible.

So if this is true, why do so many of us girls still feel the way we do? Why do we still get hurt when we're left out? Why do we spend so much time thinking about ourselves? Why do we find ourselves sucked into social media and caring so much about what we find there?

It's because we have the power to put those chains back on. We have an important choice to make. Chains or change.

If you realize you're still wearing those chains, it's time to get rid of them! Grab a Post-it note and write down something you need to have God help you get rid of. Some examples would be *self-absorption*, *insecurity*, or *comparing myself to others*. Write up as many Post-it notes as you need and then stick those little squares to yourself. Seriously! Do it! When you do, you'll discover that it's really hard to make them stick. If they do stick, they don't stay long. Get the point? You're totally done with these things!

We could keep sticking the same old Post-it notes on ourselves over and over and over again, but they're not permanent. They'll just keep falling off. It takes too much effort to keep those things attached to us!

I know it sounds silly, but do this every day if you need to. Write down the things you need God to free you from and then stick the Post-it notes on yourself as you're getting dressed, eating breakfast, riding to school, or doing your homework. As you see how easily they fall off, you'll be reminded that you're totally done with these things. They are not your identity, and they don't need to be a part of your life anymore!

As those Post-it notes fall off like a million raindrops, celebrate! When you see one fall off, stomp on it and say, "I'm not how I feel! I'm not what I struggle with! I'm not the mistakes I've made!"

You're free! You don't have to be stuck feeling bad about yourself and all the times you've messed up and made the wrong choices. Those things aren't a part of you anymore. They're in your past, and you can go ahead and leave them there. You've moved on to better things—the things God has planned for your life.

Everything's Brand New!

Just like Hosea freed Gomer, God has freed us too. We're free from all the mistakes we've made—words we wish we could take back, choices we wish we could redo, things we know we never should have done. Every single mistake!

It's like all our mistakes were written on a dry-erase board and God came in and totally erased the board. There's nothing on it anymore. It's brand new. How amazing is that?!

Now, there's something else to understand about the story of Hosea and Gomer. Hosea didn't want to just return Gomer to her rightful place as his wife. He didn't want things to just go back to the way they'd always been. No, he wanted things to be different this time. He wanted things to be even better. He wanted Gomer to sing again as she had when she and Hosea had first met—like in the early days when the two were just beginning to fall in love.

Do you remember when you first met Jesus? Maybe it was on a youth retreat or at summer camp. Perhaps one of your best friends told you about Jesus and showed you what it meant to follow Him. Or maybe you've grown up in a Christian family and Jesus was always familiar to you, yet one day you discovered who He really was and what He'd done for you, and you realized you'd never be the same again.

When I remember back to when I first met Jesus, I recall the wonder and newness of knowing Him. Everything looked so bright and meaningful! Back then it was super easy for me to keep my heart set on things above (*phroneo*, remember? Wink!) and my focus set on God. I couldn't wait to read my Bible and hear what He had to say to me. I was way more *God*-aware than *self*-aware.

But then the everydayness of life crept in, like it always does. My focus returned to *me*—what I thought of myself, what others were saying and thinking about me, what I *thought* others were saying and thinking about me. You know how it goes! You get off to such a great start by reading your Bible, doing your devotions, trying to keep your focus off yourself, and then you fizzle out. Promise and potential—*kerplunk!*—hit the wall of failure. You really want to stay close to God, but you get distracted and wander away.

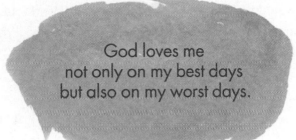

God loves me
not only on my best days
but also on my worst days.

God, though, is so faithful about bringing us back to Him. And He brings us back to Him not only on our best days but also on our worst days. He's always there!

You're All About Your Future!

When Gomer said "I do" to Hosea, she became the beloved bride—she was made brand new. Her past was overwritten by her present. And when she wandered away and ended up on the slave block, Hosea was there to rescue her (for the second time) and say, "Don't worry about your past. That's over and done with. It's all about your future now!"

God does the same thing for us. And the idea that He completes our past—that He can make everything that has ever happened to us all work out in the end—helps me understand Romans 8:28 even better. That's the verse that says God makes all things work together for the good of those who love Him. *All* things—your failures, your mistakes, your insecurities, your mess-ups, your bad choices. God takes all of that and uses every bit of it for your ultimate good!

That includes how you've treated others—and how others have treated you. How you've made your own bad decisions—and how you've followed the bad decisions of other people. How you've failed—and how others have failed you.

Hosea said that God would restore Gomer so she would go back to becoming the woman she was when she first married Hosea. The apostle Paul said that all things work together for our good. Even the prophet Job, who lost everything—his wife, his kids, his home, his money, and his health—was eventually blessed beyond everything he'd ever lost. "So the LORD blessed Job in the second half of his life even more than in the beginning" (Job 42:12 NLT).

There's a really great verse in the Bible that shows us how God can turn the mess-ups of our past into an incredible future: "You intended to harm me, but God intended it for good to accomplish what is now being done" (Genesis 50:20).

Isn't that awesome to know? Other people may intend to hurt us—when they bully us, exclude us, and don't appreciate how hard we're trying. And sometimes it's our own actions that cause the problems in our lives. But God isn't as concerned with the *cause* of our problems as He is concerned with the *cure* to our problems—His love and grace.

Your future looks amazing! That's because you're not who you were in the past. You're not all the bad things that have happened to you. You're not the bad habits you can't seem to break. You're not your insecurity. You're not someone else's opinion of you. You're not those rusty old chains that used to bind you.

You are totally loved, totally accepted, and totally complete! You are a beloved girl of God. So, tell your past where it belongs—behind you! And those old chains? They aren't the boss of you. They're like the Post-it notes that keep falling off. Let them stay on the ground where they fall and don't try to put them on ever again!

God is so wonderful. He literally will help you make peace with your past. You're a brand-new you, ready to take on the world with Jesus by your side.

Girl, it is for freedom that Jesus has set you free! Embrace the new you and the new life God has prepared for you. Toss that old test in the trash—you know, the one you didn't study for and consequently failed—open up a brand-new notebook, and discover all the amazing things God has planned for your life!

If you're trapped in insecurity,
God whispers, You are

safe in Me.

If you're stuck in an identity crisis,
God says, You are

found in Me.

If you're feeling frustrated, discontent,
or just flat-out depressed and angry,

God is still there for you!

#TheInvisibleBook

#protected

Keep vigilant watch over your
heart; that's where life starts.

—Proverbs 4:23 MSG

"Hey, Betsey! Are you coming to the party tonight?" Alex asked.

"Um...maybe," Betsey said, pulling her books out of her locker and stuffing them into her backpack.

"Why not? Everyone's going to be there!"

"Well, I might have something going on," Betsey hesitantly replied. "You know, busy weekend and all."

"Oh, come on, Betsey! It's not like you have to drink with the rest of us. I mean, you're not going to get in trouble or anything. I was kind of hoping you'd come this time."

Betsey felt herself flushing. "Oh, well, like I said, maybe."

Alex shrugged his backpack to the other shoulder. "Okay, hope to see you there!" he said before loping off down the hallway.

Betsey stood at her locker surveying the situation. On the one hand, she really wanted to hang out with Alex. She liked him. She didn't think he was a Christian, but he was nice and smart and had a great sense of humor. And let's get real. He was cute—way cute—maybe the cutest guy she'd ever seen! Just because he drank a little bit didn't mean he was a bad person.

On the other hand, she knew that kids her age shouldn't be at parties where there was drinking and all the stuff that goes along with it. But Alex seemed to be a lot nicer than some of his friends. She'd heard some stories that made her pretty nervous about going to a party with those kids.

Hoisting her backpack onto her shoulders, Betsey bit her lip. Why did things have to be so difficult? Why did she feel so conflicted about things? What was she going to do about the party?

·⁊~~⊷~⊷~~⊹·

Betsey was in a bind. Should she go to the party and not drink or not go to the party at all? Deep down she knew the right thing to do was to pass on the party, but when a guy she liked was pressuring her to go and her own mind was making excuses why it would be okay, her decision just got a whole lot harder. Betsey needed to set some boundaries in this situation, but she wasn't sure how to do that.

As Hosea walked Gomer out of the auction house the day he bought her back, he whispered, "You must live with me many days." He drew a boundary. He could give Gomer boundaries because he first drew her to him with love, not judgment. That's how a real boundary works. It's set with love and caring, and it's for the person's own good.

I have a cute little puppy named Lucy who taught me a lesson about boundaries one day. Lucy is a furry little dust mop of a creature, covered with black-and-white hair. When the weather is cold, she's content to just lie on the couch in front of the fireplace all day long. But when spring arrives, she wants to be outside. The problem is we don't have a fenced backyard. And because we know Lucy tends to wander, she's always on the end of a leash when she's outside. Most of the time a human is attached to one end.

In the spring Lucy wants to be outdoors far more than we humans have time for, and so we attach the end of her leash to various items in the backyard, including the garden hose.

One sunny day I took Lucy into the backyard, leashed her to the end of the garden hose, told her to have fun, and went back inside to get some work done.

About half an hour later, the phone rang. It was not unlike phone calls I'd received in the past. "Ma'am, I think I've found your dog." The woman went on to tell me how she'd found Lucy in her garage, attached to a loose garden hose, and with her head crammed into a bag of dog food, which she'd chewed her way through.

"Oh, my gosh! I'm so very sorry!" I gasped. Mortified, I sent my youngest son, Connor, to bring Lucy back home.

How did Lucy ever disconnect the hose? I wondered. I imagined her maneuvering her little body under the faucet, twisting herself in pretzel-like motions, and somehow managing to unscrew the hose. I went outside to investigate and discovered that the garden hose was still attached to the faucet. I was totally confused. *This would not have happened if we had a fence! This is so embarrassing!*

Soon enough along came Connor and happy-go-lucky Lucy with a leash and garden hose attached to her collar. She was too cute and tangled to scold, so I simply unattached her and sent her back inside. It was then that I discovered we actually had *two* garden hoses in the backyard—one attached to the faucet and one that had been attached to Lucy!

Lucy had wandered the neighborhood dragging a 12-foot garden hose! *The whole neighborhood must think we are the worst pet owners ever!* I thought. *Who attaches their dog to an unattached garden hose and then lets her roam the neighborhood? That does it! We're building a fence. This incident proves that Lucy needs some boundaries!*

Yes, boundaries can be restrictive, but sometimes they're a loving gift to us. They make us secure, and they prevent us from wandering away. And that's why the very first thing Hosea gave Gomer was a boundary.

Now, it's important to understand that Hosea wasn't treating Gomer like some gruff master who bosses people around. It's like what we should have done for Lucy. We should have built her a fence so she could be free to run around outdoors in the sunshine. Building a fence would have been the kindest, most thoughtful thing we could have done for her!

God wants you to see Him as a loving Father, not a gruff master. He is a fence builder desiring you to be free in the safety of His perfect plan for you. He delights in you like an artist delights in his creation. He is proud of you. He cares for you like a loving father cares for his little girl or like a knight cares for his lady. He wants to shelter you and protect you like a mother bear protects her cub. His heart for you is so much more than you could ever imagine!

> God delights in me. He is proud of me.
> He cares for me. He wants to protect me.

I think Gomer expected punishment, not love from Hosea when he bought her back. And we sometimes expect punishment when we make mistakes. We expect God to pull us out of the mess we've made, shake His head with disappointment, and then as He walks us away, give us a great big lecture.

But God always speaks to us with tenderness. He never scolds harshly. He speaks to our hearts with love. If we think of God only as a master who will punish us, then all God has is our duty and discipline. It's like how we obey a super strict teacher or coach we feel doesn't really care about us and only cares about how we perform. But God wants more than just your duty and discipline. He wants your heart.

That's why God draws us to Himself with love. And often that love shows up in the form of boundaries.

Boundaries Protect You

A famous playground experiment shows the security that boundaries bring. In the experiment a group of children was dismissed from class to go play on the playground. When a sturdy chain-link fence surrounded the school yard, the kids moved about freely, playing as if they didn't have a care in the world. But when the fence was removed, the children clumped together in small groups and stayed near the middle of the playground*.

Without boundaries the children were insecure. And without boundaries we're also insecure. When we're insecure, we start wondering things: *Am I loved? Am I worth it? Does God even see me? Am I valuable to Him?*

If Gomer didn't matter at all to Hosea, he wouldn't have set any kind of boundary for her. He wouldn't have cared enough to first redeem her and then restrict her. The boundary may have been to

---

* Robert J. Morgan, *Nelson's Complete Book of Stories, Illustrations & Quotes* [Nashville: Thomas Nelson, 2000], 592-93.

stop her from going back to her old behavior, but it was mainly to protect her heart.

God doesn't want us to be hurt by our wandering ways. His boundaries aren't there to prevent our happiness. They're there to protect our hearts.

> Boundaries are not meant to prevent my happiness—they protect my heart.

Don't Let Anything Take Away Your Heart

We were created to have, as the deepest reality in our lives, a relationship with Jesus. When we have that, everything else makes sense. Everything else flows from that relationship.

But certain things can mess up our relationship with Jesus and take away our heart. Now, we're going to get kind of personal here and talk about something that can be a big-time stumbling block to teen girls. By talking about this, I'm not condemning or judging you. I'm being honest with you and loving you with the grace and truth of Jesus.

The stumbling block we're going to talk about here is promiscuity. What's important to remember is that promiscuity isn't just an act—it's an attitude. You don't have to be in a relationship to act promiscuous. If something takes away your heart, that's promiscuity.

Think about what goes into your mind and what your eyes see. If you've ever watched a movie with scenes that would embarrass you if one of your youth leaders walked into the room, chances are that movie is taking away your heart. If you've ever read a book that caused you to think things about guys that you wouldn't want anyone else to know you're thinking, that book is taking away your heart.

There are not 50 shades of gray when it comes to this subject, my sweet little sister! It is black-and-white. If it seems gray to you, that may be because your heart has been taken. Please value yourself enough to think and pray about this. God wants to protect your heart!

It's pretty common these days to think of purity as an old-fashioned, outdated idea, but here's the deal. Purity is never, ever—no, not ever—a bad choice, and promiscuity is *always* the wrong choice. I think the biggest reason why promiscuity takes your heart is because it goes against God's perfect design of love that protects your heart.

Now, I'm aware that some of you might be feeling guilty for the choices you've made. Sweet girl, I don't condemn or judge you, but if you've dabbled with promiscuity, please read 1 John 1:9, Romans 8:1, and Isaiah 43:18-19. Confess your sin, and God will cleanse you. He doesn't ever condemn you, so please don't condemn yourself. And don't dwell on the past. Dwell in the present truth that God makes all things new! If promiscuity has taken your heart, God can give you a sparkling new, restored one.

While you're praying about this, ask God to help you establish a purity boundary. No matter how far you've gone—or not gone—into promiscuity, you never know when you're going to face temptation, so you need to have a boundary in place.

Maybe you need to start establishing a purity boundary by clearing off your bookshelf and getting rid of the books that take away your heart. Also think about the movies you watch and decide what boundary you're going to draw there. If you have a boyfriend, set a boundary to protect yourself from getting into a situation you'll regret. If you aren't in a relationship with a guy—and even if you are—ask yourself some hard questions about dating.

- What is the purpose of dating?
- What rules do I need to set for myself in this area?
- How can I keep my relationship with Jesus the number-one thing in my heart?

You also might need to consider the clothes you're wearing, the way you talk to guys, the kind of images you post of yourself online. What message are these things sending? Only you know which boundaries you need to set for yourself.

If you're unsure about some of these things, talk to a trusted friend, a parent, or a Christian woman you respect. Don't let anything take away your heart!

Boundaries That Protect

If you ask yourself just one question, ask yourself this: *How can I live with Jesus as the center of my life?*

Remember, we're all prone to wander! Even though God has redeemed us, freed us, and empowered us to be His beloved girls of God, we can still stray from Him. That's because we're human, and it's our nature to make mistakes. So, we're all going to struggle.

I don't want the spirit of promiscuity—or anything else that takes away my heart—to lead me anywhere. I want to walk with God! But when we're tempted to wander away from God and toward what we think will make us happy, we're always going to wonder who we are. That's why we need those boundaries to protect us.

Think about these things with me:

- Is what I'm doing drawing me to or away from God?
- Are the things I'm thinking about bringing me peace and joy, or are my thoughts making me feel insecure about who I am?
- Are the things I'm doing taking away my heart or drawing me closer to Jesus?

As I'm learning how to identify with my true identity and see myself as God views me, I'm learning that boundaries help me. They protect me from making mistakes and believing lies. They also help me stay close to God and remember my true identity. I've set up three important boundaries for myself, and I'd like to share them with you because I think they can help you too.

Truth

The first boundary I've set for myself is *truth*. God's Word—the Bible—is truth. If I stay within the boundary of His Word, trusting it and following it, I won't feel insecure because I'll know that the truth keeps me safe from lies I might believe or feelings that might confuse me. Psalm 119:11 says, "I have hidden your word in my heart that I might not sin against you."

That verse has many layers of meaning. First, Jesus Christ is the living Word of God. He lives within me, and His presence protects me from wandering away from Him. His written, holy Word is hidden in my heart. No matter what else is going on in my life, I have something that reminds me who I am and what I have in Christ. Psalm 119:133 also helps me focus on God: "Direct my footsteps according to your word; let no sin rule over me."

Other-Centeredness

If I stay within the boundary of *other-centeredness*, I won't feel invisible because I won't be so focused on myself. When I'm thinking of other people, I'm much happier because I'm less self-aware.

When I was a painfully self-aware teenager, especially with my white cane, my mom would always remind me to focus on others. "Look into their eyes and ask them about themselves," she would tell me. "That way all they're seeing is your caring eyes, and all they're thinking about is how kind you are to them."

My mom was right, of course! When I followed her advice, I'd temporarily forget about myself and my own problems. Philippians 2:3 says, "Do nothing out of selfish ambition or vain conceit. Rather, in humility value others above yourselves."

Accountability

My third boundary, *accountability*, is my willingness to be responsible to another person—to tell her the truth and to ask her to pray for me. When I choose to isolate myself, it's easy for me to justify the things I'm doing and not consider God or others. But my way is not always the right way! Proverbs 12:15 (NASB) says, "The way of a fool is right in his own eyes, but a wise man is he who listens to counsel."

Being accountable to someone else—like a strong Christian friend, a youth leader, or even your mom—protects you from acting out of your iddiction and also keeps you focused on the truth. Note this one teeny-weeny caution: Girls need older girls or women to be accountable to. Don't meet alone with an older boy or man in an accountability relationship. Too many weird things could happen with that. Okay? Okay.

Being accountable also means being honest, and being honest with another person requires that you be honest with yourself. James tells us to "confess your sins to one another, and pray for one another" (James 5:16 NASB). Accountability also brings encouragement. "Therefore encourage one another and build up one another" (1 Thessalonians 5:11 NASB).

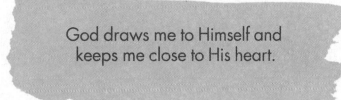

God draws me to Himself and
keeps me close to His heart.

When I'm feeling insecure or invisible or lonely or just flat-out down on myself, that's a great big clue that I've strayed from the boundaries God put in place to protect me. God's boundaries are there to protect your heart. They aren't meant to be burdens. They're meant to bring you life! They're meant to draw you closer to God.

God draws each of us to Himself through Jesus. And if we focus on Him and lift Him up, He will draw *all* of us to Himself (see John 12:32). God loves you *that* much! He loves you enough to draw you to His side with Jesus Himself. And He will keep you close because He's promised to never leave you or forsake you.

Girl, let's stay close to God's heart so nothing can ever take away our hearts. I know that you—like me—want to live like a beloved, amazing girl of God. Let's stay within the loving boundaries God has drawn for us! Let His love draw you in and keep you right next to His heart.

When you live within the boundary of truth, you'll know the

right decisions to make in life. And if you're unsure of those decisions, you'll turn to the person who is helping you be accountable,
you'll turn to God in prayer, and you *will* get answers!

When you live within the boundary of truth, you'll always know
who you are and Whose you are. You're the loved, accepted, amazing daughter of the King. You are royalty!

#know

We've covered a lot of ground in this book! I hope you're feeling encouraged. I hope you were able to relate to the stories of girls like yourself as well as the story of Gomer. I hope you're able to see yourself in a new light—the light of God's truth. And I hope you're inspired to start living out that truth!

If you and I are to live like the beloved girls of God, the only way to do this is to know Him. And that doesn't mean just knowing *about* Him. We really, really need to *know* Him.

Ultimately, it's a lack of knowledge that makes us prone to wander, and that's why knowing God is the most important action we can take to keep us from straying. Remember what happens when we wander? We become our own idol and get enslaved by sin and self.

Hosea teaches, "My people are destroyed from lack of knowledge" (Hosea 4:6). Gomer's story proves how true that is! What you don't know can hurt you, and it can also destroy you. I know that when I lack knowledge of God, my sense of identity and value are both destroyed. When I don't know who God really is, I have no idea who I am. When I'm not connected to God, my sense of security starts to slip, and my confidence disappears.

When we don't know God, it's impossible to know ourselves, and so we wander away from God to find ourselves. We find our identity in our performance. We become way too self-aware and start to compare ourselves to others. We try to get acceptance by belonging to the "right" crowd. We attempt to make up for what we see lacking in ourselves by competing with others and trying to be better than them.

But what God wants most from us isn't our perfect performance, our best behavior, or our amazing accomplishments. He wants our love. In fact God desires our loyal love for and knowledge of Him far more than He wants our sacrifices or offerings (see Hosea 6:6). Why? Because to know Him—to really, really know Him—is to love Him. And when we love Him, we don't leave Him.

Hosea 6:3 (NASB) says, "So let us know, let us press on to know the LORD. His going forth is as certain as the dawn; and He will come to us like the rain, like the spring rain watering the earth."

Girl, if you want to know who you are and live like God's beloved, you need to "press on" to know Him! And, ultimately, we know Him through His Word.

The people back in Hosea and Gomer's day chose to ignore God's Word. They didn't listen to the truth, and so they didn't really *know* the truth. And when we don't know the truth, the truth can't set us free.

You don't need to be a pastor or a youth leader or even a grown-up to know God's Word. You just need to be willing to learn! God will show you His truth in every verse if you're simply willing to open your Bible and read it. If you ignore His Word, I can guarantee you'll always feel invisible. So treat God's Word as a treasure because that's what it is. It's His gift to you. It's the way to know Him and know yourself.

When we know Jesus, we have everything! We have security. We have identity. We have value. We have satisfaction. We have confidence. We have joy. When we know Jesus, we have it all!

Really and truly!

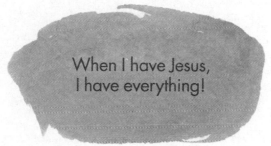

When I have Jesus,
I have everything!

And the opposite is true as well. If we don't intimately know and love God, we have nothing. And we will lack everything—security, purpose, a sense of our own value.

So as we end this book, turn to the next page of your lives and live like the beloved, amazing girls of God you are. Live with your identity in Christ instead of in an identity crisis.

I think that if Gomer could whisper something to us right now, here's what she would say: *Keep pressing in and pressing on to know God. Stay in His Word so you won't stray from His will. Never forget that you are not how you feel. Keep a right view of God, and you'll have a right view of yourself. Never overlook truth and you'll never feel invisible.*

Gomer's final words to us would probably be a lot like the final words I want to finish this book with, for they are the final words from the book of Hosea.

Who is wise? Let them realize these things.
Who is discerning? Let them understand.

The ways of the LORD are right;
the righteous walk in them,
but the rebellious stumble in them.

Hosea 14:9

Well, my new friend, that's a wrap! Thank you so much for traveling this path of freedom with me. Always remember that God loves you and His love makes you lovely. God will always be there for you. You're always visible to Him! And now go be the beloved and incredible girl of God He created you to be! I'll be praying for you.

GIFTS FROM ME TO YOU

These cute little tools will help you remember that you
are never, ever invisible to God.

— — — — — — — — — — — — — — —

God's Love Compact Mirror

Every girl needs a mirror to check her hair,
fix her lipstick, or see if she has broccoli between
her teeth! But, Gomer Girl, we need to see more
than flaws when we look in a mirror... we need
to see the truth of who we are. This magnifying
mirror is not only practical, but every time you
see yourself in its reflection, it can remind you
that you are not how you feel! As you see your
beautiful face, you can tell yourself, "God loves
me and His love makes me lovely" and "I am
not the be-tolerated or the be-perfect, I am
the beloved!" (Look in chapter 3 if you need
to remember what to see in the mirror.)

*Visit JenniferRothschild.com/Invisible and click on
"Freebies" to place your order.*
*Costs for shipping and handling will apply.
*Available only while supplies last.

Gomer Girl Manifesto

This is a must-have for me so I want
you to have it too! Download and print
this Gomer Girl Manifesto to proclaim
the truth of who you are. You can send
it to a friend, give it to your friend,
put it in your Bible, or on your mirror.
I want you to have it because I want
you to tuck these truths in your heart.

*Visit www.JenniferRothschild.com/
Invisible and click on "Freebies" to
download yours.*

Let's keep in touch...

Thank you for letting me…and Gomer…be a part of your life. I pray God has used these words to strengthen, encourage, and challenge you to believe and live out the truth that you are not how you feel!

I'd love to hear from you—literally!

Did you know I have a computer that reads my email to me? I can't promise the digital voice sounds as nice as yours, but it does allow me to hear how God is working in your life and through this book. If you'd like to contact me, send an email to **JR@jenniferrothschild.com**, or better yet, go to the "contact us" link at **www.JenniferRothschild.com/Invisible**.

While you're there, sign up to receive Java with Jennifer. That way, we can stay connected over coffee every Friday! It's my blog that you'll get in your inbox. My hope is that I can pour some encouragement into your life and we can grow stronger and wiser from each other.

If you're on Facebook, find me at facebook.com/Jennifer.J.Rothschild.
If you tweet, I'm @jennrothschild.
On Instagram, you can locate me @jennrothschild.
And, of course, on Pinterest, I am jennrothschild.

And for those of you who actually still write letters—you know, with pen and paper, envelopes, and stamps—you can find me at:
4319 S. National Ave., Suite 303, Springfield, MO 65810

Well, Gomer Girl, you matter to me and you matter to God. I may be blind, but I can see your incredible beauty and value—I hope you see it too!

Love,

Jennifer

Other Great Resources from Jennifer Rothschild

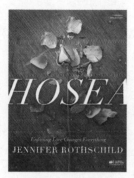

Hosea: Unfailing Love Changes Everything

In this 7-session DVD driven study, you'll experience the love story of Hosea and Gomer; God and Israel. And, you'll discover it's your love story too! We're all like Gomer—deeply loved, but prone to wander—seeking acceptance and identity in all the wrong places. Through Hosea, Jennifer Rothschild will teach you how to know your God, know your identity, and live out your beautiful story.

Lessons I Learned in the Dark: Steps to Walking by Faith, Not by Sight

At the age of fifteen, Jennifer Rothschild confronted two unshakable realities: Blindness is inevitable...and God is enough. Now this popular author, speaker, and recording artist offers poignant lessons that illuminate a path to freedom and fulfillment. With warmth, humor, and insight, Jennifer shares the guiding principles she walks by—and shows you how to walk forward by faith into God's marvelous light.

**Me, Myself, and Lies:
A Thought Closet Makeover**

Adapted from the trade book *Self Talk, Soul Talk*, in the Bible Study *Me, Myself and Lies* Jennifer shares practically and helpfully from her own life and from Scripture to show how every woman can turn her words—and her life—around for good.

This six-week Bible study for women encourages them to clean out the junk in their thoughts and replace these hidden negative thoughts and failures with positive truths from God's Word. Rather than struggling with self-esteem, body image, stress, and other unhealthy thoughts and emotions, they can learn to replace the lies they may have been telling themselves with the truth from God's Word.

www.JenniferRothschild.com